Daniel

A portrait of Russia 15 years ago.
Curious about your rx.
to it.

HOT ICE:
SHAKESPEARE IN MOSCOW
A Director's Diary

by
Guy Sprung
with Rita Much

Thanks for your
support (again)

Looking forward to
getting to know you
some more.

HOT ICE

SHAKESPEARE IN MOSCOW

A DIRECTOR'S DIARY
BY GUY SPRUNG
WITH RITA MUCH

Blizzard Publishing • Winnipeg

First published in 1991
by Blizzard Publishing
301–89 Princess Street
Winnipeg, Canada R3B 1K6

© 1991 Guy Sprung & Rita Much

Cover design by Terry Gallagher
Back cover photo by Sylvia Paccotta
Printed in Canada for Blizzard Publishing
by Hignell Printing Limited.

Published with the assistance of the Canada Council
and the Manitoba Arts Council.

This publication is fully protected under the copyright laws of Canada and all other
countries of the Copyright Union and is subject to royalty.

All rights reserved. No part of this book (including cover design) may be reproduced or
transmitted in any form, by any means, electronic or mechanical, including photocopying,
recording, and information storage and retrieval systems, without permission in writing
from the publisher, except in the case of quotations embodied in critical articles and
reviews.

All quotations from *A Midsummer Night's Dream* are from
The Riverside Shakespeare © 1974 by Houghton Mifflin Company.

Canadian Cataloguing in Publication Data

Sprung, Guy, 1947–

   Hot ice
   ISBN 0-921368-18-6

1. Sprung, Guy, 1947- - Diaries. 2. Shakespeare, William, 1564-1616. Midsummer
night's dream. 3. Shakespeare, William, 1564-1616 - Dramatic production.
4. Shakespeare, William, 1564-1616 - Stage history - Soviet Union - Moscow. I. Much,
Rita, 1954-. II. Title.

PN2308.S678A3 1991   792.9/2   C91-097093-9

To the cast and crew of the Pushkin Theatre,
with admiration and gratitude.
And to my partner, Rita, whose idea this was.

Acknowledgements

This book was completed with the assistance of the
Canada Council and the Ontario Arts Council. We would
also like to express our gratitude to Peter Atwood and
Gordon Shillingford at Blizzard Publishing, as well as to
David Black, the Canadian Embassy in Moscow, Sylvia
Paccotta, ECS Group of Companies, Tamara Galko, Assia
DeVreeze, and Valery Fomin.

CONTENTS

———————

Photographs from the production appear after page 72.

Merry and tragical? Tedious and brief?
That is hot ice and wondrous strange snow.
How shall we find the concord of this discord?
    (Theseus, *A Midsummer Night's Dream*, Act V, scene i)

Cast and Crew of the Pushkin Theatre Production
of Shakespeare's *A Midsummer Night's Dream*

Theseus, Duke of Athens	Valery Barinov
Egeus, father to Hermia	Valentin Burov
Lysander	Andrey Dubovsky
Demetrius	Alexander Borovikov
Philostrate, Master of the Revels to Theseus	Andrey Shiriayev
Hippolyta, Queen of the Amazons	Elena Skorokhodova
Hermia, daughter to Egeus	Maria Andreeva
Helena	Irina Biakova
Oberon, King of the Fairies	Alexander Yermakov
Titania, Queen of the Fairies	Maria Zubareva
Puck or Robin Goodfellow	Sergei Agapitov
Quince, a carpenter	Yuri Rumiantcev
Bottom, a weaver	Vasilij Funtikov
Flute, a bellows-mender	Vladimir Grigorev
Snout, a tinker	Victor Vasiliev
Snug, a joiner	Vitaliyi Edininskov
Starveling, a tailor	Nina Marushina

Fairies and soldiers played by the first-year students
of the Moscow Art Theatre School

Director	Guy Sprung
Assistant Director	Andrey Shiriayev
Stage Manager	Elena Shumskaya
Composer	Arkady Serper
Set design by	Valery Fomin
Costumes by	Ksenia Shemanovskaya
Choreography by	Tatyana Borisova and Sergei Tsvetkov

THE WARM-UP

Introduction

There's nothing in the world better than Moscow. Let us go!
(Chekhov's The Three Sisters, *Act III)*

The Road to Moscow

In the fall of 1984 when I was the Artistic Director of the Toronto Free Theatre, I got a phone call from someone asking me if I would like to meet a group of Russian theatre artists who were in town to see something of Canadian theatre. How I was chosen for this encounter, I don't know, but I went down to the offices of the Russia-Canada Friendship Society on Queen Street West with mild curiosity. The exterior of the building is reasonably familiar to the few Canadians who watch CBC, because the series "Street Legal" used to use the frontage for its title and credit sequences. Like any true Canadian with maple syrup in his veins, I looked for the hidden KGB cameras as I mounted the stairs. What followed was a pleasant couple of hours talking theatre shop over vodka with five Russians, half a dozen Canadians and a translator. Our "team" included actress Fiona Reid, director George Luscombe, who was still running Toronto Workshop Productions at the time, and a couple of other directors besides myself. The Russian "team" was made up of an actress, a critic, a publisher, the head of the Russian branch of the International Theatre Institute and the head of GITIS,[1] Russia's national theatre school. No earth-shattering cultural exchange took place, but some genuine Canadian niceness was swapped for some guarded Russian friendliness. They politely assumed that theatre in Canada was still in its infancy while Russian theatre, steeped in craft and tradition, was the best in the world. The leader of their group was clearly the round-faced, squat, powerful man from GITIS. It was whispered

---

[1] State Institute of Theatre and Cinema.

around the table that he was a former Minister of Culture; the suggestion was that we were supposed to be flattered we were in the presence of such a high-ranking delegation. I've forgotten his name. He chain-smoked through the whole discussion from a pile of cigarettes on the table in front of him. They weren't in any package. Were they western cigarettes and was he too embarrassed to admit to a preference for capitalist commodities? He lit each cigarette carefully with a yellow disposable lighter, the Russian imitation of a Bic, no doubt. The thumb of the hand he used to light his cigarettes had a small polyp, a little protrusion of flesh, perfectly formed through constant use to catch the flint wheel of the lighter and make the continuous lighting of his smokes easier. While he droned on about the extraordinary virtues of theatre in Russia I watched in fascination as the little protrusion lit cigarette after cigarette. I was hooked. I had to visit Russia.

The meeting ended with the inevitable toasts to Russian-Canadian friendship and international co-operation. I stood up and made some slightly smart-ass remark about how lucky they are as theatre artists because theatre in their country is so respected and its power so feared that scripts are censored, whereas in our country theatre is so unimportant that our "authorities" don't care what we put on the stage. The humour of my remark was not appreciated, nor was my genuine intent understood. During the goodbyes I stated I would be coming to the Soviet Union for a visit in the near future. They nodded politely and handed me a present, a souvenir collection of matchboxes decorated with Russian landscapes and stuffed with tiny matches, very few of which actually lit when struck.

Until this encounter my knowledge of and contact with the Soviet Union had been no more than that of the average Canadian. I watched in awe the extraordinary skill of the artists of the Moscow Circus performing at Maple Leaf Gardens. I cursed when they beat us at hockey, at the same time marvelling at the intelligence and craft the Russians applied to the game. I remember a short documentary on Tretiak, their brilliant goalie and one of the main reasons they beat us so often in the '70s and '80s. It was one of those TV profiles that separates beer commercials between periods. I remember, in particular, a shot of Tretiak juggling tennis balls to develop his hand-eye co-ordination. If this is what hockey players do to train, I wondered, what might actors do? While developing a collective play in Saskatchewan in 1978 called *Paper Wheat*, about the opening up of the Canadian prairies, I had worked with a Ukrainian-Canadian actor and encouraged him to create some scenes in Ukrainian. In the show he sang a beautiful, tear-jerking song. "We are only happy when we are sad," he was fond of saying, wiping a tear from his eye with a grin. Does this "concord in discord" apply to Russians as well? I wondered. It was six months later, in April of 1985, when I finally found the time and scraped together the money to make my first visit to Moscow, the capital of a country Russians themselves love to refer to as a *Zagadka*, a riddle or enigma.

This first visit was short—eight days—and devoted exclusively to watching and talking theatre.[2] I was lucky. A fellow director from Toronto, Jonathan McKenzie, had just come back from a year in Moscow, where he studied the language and the theatre. He helped me bone up on life in Russia and gave me the names of a few "unofficial" contacts to look up. On the evening I arrived I somehow managed to make a public phone box work and reached one of Jonathan's friends. ("Don't use the hotel phone. It is tapped," everyone had said.) The friend spoke English, as Jonathan had promised. "Come on over. We are having a wedding," she said, so I spent my first night in Moscow crammed into a tiny room with twenty-five people celebrating the marriage of a couple who had already been living together for years with the husband's parents and had one child. They finally had been granted an apartment and could now get married.[3] Vodka, politics and theatre until three in the morning. I thought I had died and gone to heaven.

My memory of that first visit is of being in a state of continual mental overdrive, of watching plays in a language I didn't understand and talking non-stop in French or German or, occasionally, English to an ever-expanding circle of Russian acquaintances until the early hours of the morning, and then cabbing or walking back to the hotel through the dark streets of Moscow. Gorbachev had only just come to power and the "official" government bureaucrats running the theatres and theatre organizations were still cautious and stodgy in their relations with westerners. In stark contrast, the younger network of actors, directors and writers that I had been introduced to through Jonathan's friends was relishing the new-found freedom to talk and exchange ideas. It was still against the law to have a westerner in a private home without police permission, and theoretically they could be arrested if a militiaman came to the door and found me. This

[2] See Appendix A.
[3] If a couple got married before securing an apartment, chances are the State would assume they didn't need one.

didn't bother them in the slightest. They were riding the wave of social, political and cultural transformation with euphoric abandon. A westerner was still a novelty and the object of everything from curiosity to opportunism. One was passed from one circle of friends to the next. Many were trying to take advantage of the political climate to leave the country. A few hopeful single moms even paraded their kids in front of me during the course of the week. Others were desperately trying to trace any Jewish blood in their family history in order to qualify for visas to Israel. The bride and groom I met on that first evening are living in Toronto now. The groom's first job was selling hot dogs at the corner of Yonge and King.

Moscow theatres in 1985 were packed. There were always long line-ups for returns and every time I approached a theatre I was accosted by hungry would-be theatre-goers asking me if I had any spare tickets. It was a little like running the gauntlet of scalpers at the Forum in Montreal. My excitement as a first-time visitor to Moscow, along with the brewing tension in the souls of the audience as they tried to deal with their confusion, hopes and apprehension about the coming changes in their country, combined to create for me the experience of enthralling theatre. Three productions stand out in my memory as emblematic of the times.

Two of them were at the Theatre on the Taganka and directed by Yuri Lyubimov, one of the towering figures in contemporary Russian theatre. His *Tartuffe* was a free reworking of Molière's text which focussed on some of the censorship problems the author had experienced in producing theatre in seventeenth-century France. Of course, it was a barely veiled statement about the current censorship in the Soviet Union. One could not help being struck by the cynical ability with which the actors strutted their craft, reinforced, no doubt, by the fact that the play had been in the repertoire for twenty years. Some of the play, inexplicably, was in French and the actors demonstrated an agility with the language which would shame most Canadian actors in our "bilingual" country.

Lyubimov's final production in his own theatre, Chekhov's *The Three Sisters*, was also his most controversial. The official censor in the Ministry of Culture had the power and responsibility to alter or cut the text of any production a theatre proposed to mount, but of course you wouldn't dare touch Chekhov. Lyubimov, with only a little judicious chopping and inverting of the text, was able to make the "father of modern Russian drama" speak directly to contemporary Russians. All references in the original to the approaching end of the Czarist era became, through changes in the imagery, references to the coming end of the Stalinist legacy in Russia. The costumes were a clever mixture of *fin de siècle* and modern fashion. The artillery band only referred to in the play was actually seen when a part of one of the walls in the auditorium opened up to reveal a Red Army band playing one of their schmaltzy favourites. Olga's famous speech at the end of the play, "our sufferings will turn into joy for those who live after us, happiness and peace will come to this earth," became a speech about the hopes of the audience watching the show. They devoured the message hungrily. Apparently, Lyubimov had opened the production and then immediately gone into exile. The authorities kept his productions in the repertoire; all they did was take his name out of the program. Neither production had a director's credit.

Like *Tartuffe*, *The Three Sisters* was directed with a profound distrust of any emotional involvement. Lines were shouted at the audience, lights flashed seemingly at random throughout scenes, and the house lights came on constantly in the middle of speeches. As one whole side of the auditorium was covered with a huge mirror, the audience spent a good deal of time watching itself watching the performance. Why are the Soviets so distrustful of engaging the audience? This was a manifestation of Brecht's theories exaggerated to ludicrous proportions. The consensus among the younger generation of theatre artists was that the authorities had consciously allowed theatre to become the cultural canary down the coal mine of Soviet society, in order to test the air of political dissension while allowing the intellectuals to vent a little political steam. Lyubimov had overstepped the unwritten limits and so had been "allowed" to go into exile.

The significant third production came from Tbilisi in Georgia. The Rustavelli Company, run by Robert Stura, was known internationally for producing plays that examined the nature of tyranny (like a version of *Richard III* they had taken to the Edinburgh Festival). Their new play, *Judgement Day*, seemed to me to have a very mushy core, but on the surface it was a blatant attack on the legacy of Stalin. It was in Georgian, so the theatre provided simultaneous translation for the Muscovites. The message must have been deemed too seditious for 1985; a friend was quick to point out that the Russian coming through the headphones was a sanitized version of the Georgian text spoken by the actors. Gorbachev had seen the production in a special matinée. I wonder how his Georgian is.

Thus theatre at the dawn of *perestroika* was pushing at the limits of intellectual freedom, serving both as an indication of a need and as a fuel for the engine of change. It had energy and a function, and was desperately important to the spectator. It was to a very different Moscow that I returned four years later as a guest of the Union of Theatre Workers and a delegate to an international symposium on Stanislavsky. I had kept up a little contact with the Soviet Union in the interim, but I had been mainly preoccupied with founding the Canadian Stage Company, an amalgamation of my own Toronto Free Theatre and Bill Glassco's CentreStage. The need for a large company in Toronto devoted to developing and showcasing the best of Canadian theatre seemed to me self-evident and so I had pushed and pulled a very phlegmatic Glassco into making it happen. It had been four years of sweat and torture, and this mid-winter visit to Moscow was a welcome mental oasis in a period of building a theatre that was costing me more effort than it should have.

During those four years *glasnost* and *perestroika* had dominated the world media. We in the west had begun to revere the man who had both the wisdom and the courage to end the Cold War. But in Moscow hope had begun to turn to despondency. Gorbachev was not the hero he was outside his own country.

The symposium of three hundred-odd theatre specialists, academics and artists from around the world felt suspiciously as though it had been organized by the Russians as a massive PR gesture. It was so gloriously disorganized it soon degenerated into something akin to a lovable farce, valuable more for the informal chats than the official sessions.

Peter Brook addressed the delegates on the dialectical evolution of theatrical theories. He carefully expressed his reverence for the theories of Stanislavsky while insisting on their need to be overhauled and recharged. It was more a political tightrope walk, making sure he offended no one, than it was a serious thesis. He came across as an amiable, aging Englishman with a charming smile and the air of an Indian guru. As a university student I had revered his first book on theatre, *The Empty Space*. But I had been puzzled by his latest production of Chekhov's *The Cherry Orchard*, which I had seen at the Brooklyn Academy of Music in New York. This same production arrived for a very limited number of performances as an adjunct to the conference. Those Russians who managed to see it were privately quite disparaging, particularly in their comparison of it to the Peter Stein version of *The Three Sisters* that the Schaubuehne of Berlin had brought to Moscow only one month earlier.

Lyubimov also spoke, or rather, was crowned at the conference. The authorities had only recently given him permission to return to Russia and a standing ovation greeted his entrance on the stage. Stanislavsky, he claimed, had never been much of an influence on him. Brecht and Meyerhold had been his gods. Stanislavsky, of course, had at one time been equated with the State-approved performance aesthetic of socialist realism. How much of the conference was an attempt by artists to distance themselves from the past while rescuing Stanislavsky from the stigma of Stalinism, I don't know. When I questioned one of the Russian participants at the conference on the phenomenon of Lyubimov, he answered with quiet intensity, "He was there for us when we needed him." Now he has his own theatre back, his name will go back on the programs and he will once again be able to play his part in the future of the great *Zagadka*.

In the four years I'd been away theatre in Moscow had gone crazy. As many as forty fringe theatres had sprung up, playing in any available large room or small hall all over the city. The Ministry of Culture no longer censored scripts or controlled the repertoire of the various theatres and even started to hand out small grants to some of these new fringe theatres. Original plays portraying drunks and prostitutes and other sides of Soviet life that had been taboo on the stage until recently were being gobbled up. New western plays were being translated almost overnight. The atmosphere was a curious mixture of a frenzied creative energy and despondency about the future of the country, a despondency which I was to come to understand in my next visits.

Through a chain of meetings that started with Jonathan McKenzie's original circle of friends I met Yury Yeremin, the Artistic Director of the Pushkin Theatre in Moscow, who asked me to direct something for his theatre. I suggested Richard Greenblatt[4] direct Robert Fothergill's *Detaining Mr. Trotsky* which had premièred successfully at the Toronto Free Theatre and which I had had translated into Russian. It is about Trotsky's imprisonment in Nova Scotia during his journey back to Russia before the October Revolution. Yury was not the slightest bit interested in having Trotsky on his stage. "We don't want those politics any more," he said. I then tried to interest him in *Quiet in the Land*, Anne Chislett's play about the Amish in southern Ontario during WWI, a brilliant father/son drama about the responsibilities of technology. It sounded too pro-German for Yury's liking. We started to talk about Shakespeare. The Bard had not been

---

[4] Associate Artistic Director of Toronto Free Theatre at the time.

done recently in Moscow. I talked about some of the early plays I had directed. Later, Yury was to see in a Soviet digest of western theatre a few pictures of the production of *A Midsummer Night's Dream* I had staged in Vancouver. He wanted that. I said I would think about it and get in touch with him when I got back to Canada. We agreed the best way to proceed was for me to come back some time in the fall to begin preliminary discussions. I left his office buzzing.

This visit to Moscow ended with the theatre in Saratov, a city on the Volga, trying to get me to come to see some of their productions. The Karl Marx Theatre there had been described to me as the home of the most stylistically exciting theatre happening anywhere in Russia. I wanted to see what they were doing and perhaps bring a show back to Canada. The city was technically off-limits to foreigners, a "closed" city, because it is situated in the heart of the industrial district of Russia. Nevertheless the Karl Marx Theatre got permission for my visit from the local KGB general. They also bribed a friendly Aeroflot pilot to get me on an airplane and they even went so far as to change their repertoire so that my visit would coincide with their best productions. However, they never got the KGB headquarters in Moscow to permit my visit. After one week of attempting to stick-handle through the superbly inefficient bureaucracy, they admitted defeat, but not without leaking the story to *Isvestia*, in conjunction with the Theatre Union, of official KGB intransigence. After my departure this became a front-page story about the KGB sabotaging international cultural exchanges.[5]

With the PanAm flight rolling down the runway I felt the usual relief of having escaped Soviet Immigration and Customs without being arbitrarily arrested. But as the passengers cheered on take-off I felt a growing excitement about the possibility of doing a Shakespeare in Russian.

Bottom: ... our play is preferr'd.
(A Midsummer Night's Dream, *Act IV, scene ii*)

The Road to *A Midsummer Night's Dream*

A theatre director is a hybrid artistic calling whose role in the process of play production has been accepted as necessary only over the last one hundred years. The "art" of a theatre director is such a convoluted

[5] See Appendix B.

concoction that it is impossible to dissect it into its components. We are part interpretative, part creative artist, with generous helpings of diplomat, politician, business person, venture capitalist, technician and con-artist stirred in. We are watchers, not doers. Without a predominant talent to write or act, we harness our drive to communicate by orchestrating the talents and craft of others. A theatre director is a phenomenon worthy of a chapter in one of those trendy books on chaos and the underlying principles of the universe—right after the chapter on snowflakes as non-equilibrium phenomena.[6]

Becoming a theatre director wasn't even in the outer orbit of my mind when I was collecting awards as the high school jock or enrolling in university to become an archaeologist. Nobody in our family had the remotest interest in theatre. My contact with it was limited to rare encounters as a spectator. But now, as I mentally flip through the images of those early experiences, I realize that I never had any choice in the matter. Somehow, somewhere, something was guiding me, as if I were a human Exocet missile, to the calling of using theatre as a can opener on the great can of worms that is life. My father was a Winnipeg boy who got his PhD in philosophy on a scholarship in Berlin before the war. My mother was a German who hated the way German men treated their women and so found herself a foreigner. Dad joined the Canadian Army when the war broke out and stayed on after it ended. So I grew up a "military brat." There are a lot of us in Canadian theatre. Pop psychology might have it that we moved around so much as children we never developed a sense of "home" and consequently we had no consistent sense of "self." Theatre lets us look for "self" in "action." Well, maybe. As a product of a prairie philosopher-cum-army officer and a German immigrant, I should be forgiven if my approach to theatre ended up on the serious side. Theatre to me is one of the last great secular mysteries.

When I was eleven my father was the Canadian Military Attaché in Sweden. My parents sent me to a school in northern Germany in an effort to have me learn my "mother tongue," as it were. The school was situated on a farm and had one of those spartan regimes requiring its students to go for a run and take a cold shower before breakfast. It was summer when I arrived and soon after I got there the senior students put on an outdoor production of *A Midsummer Night's Dream* in German. I remember clearly the moment one of my classmates told me about the event. As someone

[6] Products of imbalance in the flow of energy from one piece of nature to another.

who spoke English, I was expected to know the works of Shakespeare backwards. And of course, I'd never heard of him. I recall the boy saying, "He is one of your writers." This puzzled me for a while as I thought he meant Shakespeare was a Canadian. Naturally I bluffed and pretended to know all about this great "Canadian." The play was staged in the woods just a few minutes' walk from the school. The audience sat on the grass under the trees. I tagged along with the other junior students expecting, with true Ontario philistinism, the evening to be boring culture, sissy stuff. Whammo! I was riveted. I was enthralled. I tried desperately to parry this enthralment with skepticism. No chance. I went back and saw every performance, embarrassed to the point that I had to slink away from my classmates without telling them where I was going.

If I met some of those student actors now, thirty years later, I'm convinced I'd recognize them. Wall (Snout) was a tall, lanky student who performed the part with a disdainful drawl. He made the "crannied hole or chink" by holding out his arm as if to shake some invisible hand and splitting apart his third and second fingers, the way kids do to test their muscle coordination. It is difficult for me to see Wall any other way.[7]

Other early images of theatre are registered equally indelibly in the computer of my memory. This should have told me something but I wasn't listening. I fled high school to take anthropology at McGill only to find that after the first few months my professors' boredom with what they were teaching had successfully killed my own enthusiasm. I needed something more committed, more passionate. By accident (as I thought at the time) I stumbled into the university student drama club. Dabbling in acting, producing and directing, I was lured deeper and deeper into the magic of theatre, resisting all the while the possibility that it might be a serious calling. With each attempt on my part to pull myself loose from its hold, theatre, like some giant spider's web, would only entangle me further. Twenty years later I am still exploring the limits of the stage as the elemental medium of human intercourse.

Theatre's ability to tell stories, capture character and manifest the unending range of the human imagination is infinite. When theatre is great it reaches inside us and sets the molecules of our souls vibrating. The actors are alive, the sweat is real, and while the spilt blood is only artificial or even merely symbolic, we as audience members actively throw our imagination

[7] Yes, the original Wall in the Moscow production was tall and lanky, and performed with a disdainful drawl.

at the stage and choose to join in the deception. We participate in a performance as members of a collective of watchers and our participation is an integral part of the chemistry and magic of the event.[8] Film and video thrust their illusions upon us and are immune to any reaction from us. We watch these illusory media in the loneliness of our own imaginings. Theatre is one of the few weapons people have in the struggle against what Northrop Frye calls "the internalizing and individualizing effects of technology."[9] Theatre is also one of the few weapons we Canadians have left to help us carve out a sense of self-worth in this increasingly homogeneous world. The financial benefits of the art will always remain so negligible that our economic masters to the south will, I hope, never feel they have to control our theatre the way they control our television and movie screens. The more contemporary theatre escapes from the cul-de-sac of trying to outdo the camera's capacity for recreating a realistic impression of reality, the more it rediscovers, in verbal poetry and visual metaphor, its own strong suit. The camera, film and video, has forced theatre to become more like theatre.

And then there is Shakespeare.

Though his wordcraft was so extraordinary that he affected the development of the English language itself, he never participated in any attempt to preserve his work for posterity. Words for the Bard were merely a blueprint used by a company of actors to transform themselves into the real thing: a ceremony, a happening, a telepathic collective experience—the live performance that transcends the mere text. Never before or since has one person coupled such an extraordinary wordcraft with an understanding of theatre gained from the experience of being an actor, director[10] and shareholder. He was able to elevate theatre into a metaphor for life itself.

Driven to recreate the enthralment I felt when I first saw *A Midsummer Night's Dream*, in the summer of 1983 with the help of the City of Toronto Parks Department and Andrey Tarasiuk,[11] I founded a yearly outdoor Shakespeare event in High Park. We transformed a sloping hill with a grove of oak trees at its base into one of the most magical sites

[8] In French, instead of going to see a play you "*assister à*" or "assist" the play. Shakespeare's uncanny understanding of the workings of theatre and in particular of the chemistry between the audience and the actors is what determines the playing of the monologues.

[9] Northrop Frye on CBC's "Ideas," November 1990.

[10] For the Bard's ironic statement on the role of the playwright as director we need only look at Quince in *A Midsummer Night's Dream*.

[11] Now the Artistic Director of Theatre Direct, Toronto.

possible for the play. I cast the play and hired the artistic teams, but in a mistaken assumption that it might be better for the project if I were free to handle all the concomitant problems of working out of doors at a new location, I decided not to direct it myself. But the director quit ten days before the opening (citing technical chaos as his reason), so in an atmosphere of impending catastrophe, and with the enormous input of R.H. Thomson, I stepped in to push the project through. Artists and technicians alike reached down inside themselves and dragged out unusual resources. The result was a tremendous crowd-pleaser. "The Dream in High Park," as we subsequently dubbed the venture, has developed into a permanent venue for outdoor Shakespeare.

Since Peter Brook did his famous production at the Royal Shakespeare Company in the late '60s, *A Midsummer Night's Dream* has never been the same. He destroyed for ever the clichéd Victorian notion of the fairies as sweet little creatures dancing in rings at the end of the garden. In doing so he opened the play up to rediscovery by future generations and was a seminal influence in widening the permissible bounds of Shakespeare interpretation. Thanks to Brook, directors in the English-speaking world have been granted the right to attack the canon with a greater breadth of imagination. I was lucky enough to catch the production during its final run at the Aldwych Theatre in London. In retrospect I think it was a little reticent in exploring some of the darker aspects of the play, a kind of "No Sex, Please, We're British" version.

A Midsummer Night's Dream is one of the Bard's most frequently produced plays and I've seen numerous other versions, of course. One at the National Theatre School in Montreal in the late '60s (pre-Brook) used hundreds of green garbage bags, which were a novelty then, to create the set. In the late '70s Henry Tarvainen, also at the NTS, borrowed much of Brook's acrobatic approach but actually started to look at the male-female conflict in the piece a little more seriously. In High Park in 1983 the real star of the production was nature herself. The words had a unique focus and magic as the shadows lengthened and deliquesced into pitch black. The air, the trees, the moon added resonance to the event. The Elizabethan mechanicals were successfully time-travelled to the Toronto of the day, and worked well with broad "MacKenzie Brothers" accents. In many ways we are lucky to be able to approach the Bard with Canadian accents. English actors, for example, the Royal Shakespeare Company, often feel trapped, as they themselves admit, in a King's English, the received middle-class pronunciation that became dominant well after Shakespeare was in his grave. By a quirk of linguistic history, Canadian English may be closer to the actual pronunciation of Elizabeth I than is the speech of Elizabeth II.

At the Vancouver Playhouse in 1987 I tackled the play from start to finish as the director for the first time. There I started to explore the sexual undertones of the forest, and the proximity of the comedy to tragedy. Oberon accompanied many of his monologues on a bass guitar. (Imagine "I know a bank where the wild thyme blows" as a modern rap song.) But what had sounded in the rehearsal hall like a feasible idea collapsed under the weight of technical ambition and lack of on-stage rehearsals. Much of what I tried to do in Moscow was based on what did and did not work in Vancouver. As I said, it was the photographs from that production, combined with a write-up in a Soviet digest of western theatre, that intrigued Yury Yeremin enough to want a similar production for his theatre. Presumably nothing stylistically like the leather costumes of the forest fairies had been seen in Russia before.

Why should I do a Shakespeare in Russia now? Why should I do *A Midsummer Night's Dream* now? (Yes, even the Bard needs a reason for being staged.) As a Canadian directing a play in a Russia embroiled in a chaotic but so far quiet revolution, I needed to be clear about what I was doing. There were plenty of good selfish reasons, including the possibility that if I were to set up the contacts with this project, then eventually, when I felt the time was right and we had the work to show off, I would take the Canadian Stage Company to the Pushkin Theatre on tour.

I was also fascinated and frightened by the potential relevance of the play to Moscow in 1990. The proximity of Soviet Russia to the horror and violence of the Second World War and Stalinism, the boiling civil and ethnic unrest, would allow the Russians a very different access to the text than an audience in a comfortable and contented Toronto or Vancouver. On one level the play is very much about the revenge of the subconscious on the conscious world. How does one stage this in a country that is trying to come to grips with over seventy years of officially pretending the subconscious doesn't exist? Theseus's Athens in *A Midsummer Night's Dream* is a circumlocution for Shakespeare's London. Could it also be one for Gorbachev's Moscow?

Do I have the right as an *inostranetz* ("foreigner") to even think these thoughts? Is a Canadian directing in Moscow right now an oxymoron—hot ice?

FIRST PERIOD

Meeting the Company

Sunday, October 8, 1989

Quince: This green plot shall be our stage, this hawthorn brake our tiring-house, (Act III, scene i)

The week before leaving for Moscow was sheer madness. The Canadian Stage Company, with one show already running in Edmonton and three openings in Toronto within the previous eight days, all launched with a tiny support staff headed by a floundering General Manager, was threatening to blow a fuse. One of the openings, Sally Clark's new play, *The Trial of Judith K.*, got the kind of reviews guaranteed to keep audiences away in droves. Not the best way to start the season for a theatre company that last year had an operating loss of one and a half million dollars. Nor a great way for me to begin my first season as Producing Artistic Director. In truth, the production lost some of the humour that had been present in readings and workshops when the script was being developed.

On Thursday and Friday the English Stage Company's productions of *Our Country's Good* and *The Recruiting Officer* opened. By the time I left yesterday only *The Globe and Mail* review had appeared. Ray Conlogue liked *Our Country's Good*, thank God, but the review was buried in the Saturday section and won't get noticed. And Ray, true to form, tried to demonstrate his intellectual superiority to the minds that shaped the production and in so doing patronized the work. It's not a review that will help much at the box office. What will the *Toronto Star* say? We desperately need a big hit to start the season. How disgustingly humiliating to have to rely so heavily on what the critics say for our survival. Russian theatre doesn't have *this* problem.

The visit of the Royal Court has given an odd taste to the top of our season. While *The Recruiting Officer* is merely an acceptable production, *Our Country's Good* is a stunning example of the power of theatre itself. I brought the company over as a challenge to theatre in this city, to the Canadian Stage and to myself. This is great theatre and, given the time and the support, we can do as well and better. Unfortunately, my throwing down the theatrical gauntlet was taken as a hostile gesture by many. Actors' Equity even sent an official letter decrying the inclusion of the British company in our season as "detrimental to Canadian theatre." The cast of our own show, *Judith K.*, is probably envious of the "royal" treatment the English actors are getting. A meeting with the marketing department determined that we will very likely have to close the Sally Clark play because of poor ticket sales.[1]

If the Royal Court shows aren't a success will the theatre go under? The tighter the financial situation the less room we have to stick-handle our way out of our deficit. Certainly there will be no freedom to deal with the problem of the General Manager. I talked privately with a few of the board members and each advised me that now was not the time to try to change management at the theatre. While desperately trying to tie up the loose ends before leaving for Moscow, I wondered whether in fact I should be going at all. Can I afford the time away from Canada now? I hope my absence for eight days will prove to be a short-term risk for the long-term benefits of building bridges outside the country.

Air Canada was once again late getting off the ground, and the service must now be the worst of any airline in the world. The steak would have made a hockey puck feel soft. One of the many benefits of Mulroney's drive to privatization?

Ken Dryden was on the leg from Frankfurt to Moscow. He is on his way to Russia to shoot one episode of a documentary series on hockey. A quiet giant of a man. I pity anybody sitting next to him on planes—his shoulders push out half-way into the adjoining seats. We met fifteen years ago while working together on a play about the Montreal Canadiens. I had suggested his name as a prospective board member to the nominating committee at the Canadian Stage only to have the corporate types roll their eyes. Dryden quite likes theatre and often takes his children to theatre in Toronto. I fished around a little and got the impression that if asked he might be prepared to serve on the board. I suspect he has the kind of

[1] We did close it early and the actors objected publicly.

intelligence mixed with community concern that would help the theatre a lot. He talked about the challenges the Soviet hockey system was experiencing with *peristroika*.

Yanina Godsulskaya, a Toronto actress with a Russian background, was hired by the Pushkin to work on the production as an interpreter. I wanted someone in my corner who knew my work as a director to help unravel some of the complexities of the situation rather than an "official" interpreter with an agenda I didn't understand. Yanina knew immediately when the plane started to fly over the Soviet Union. "All the roads go like this," she explained, making a movement with her hands like a snake wriggling along the ground.

At Immigration one still has the feeling of being defenceless prey venturing into the jaws of the Russian bear. I tried to grin my most innocent "I'm just a Canadian director, I'm not a spy" smile. Since the visit in February the Soviets have renovated. Now a duty-free store awaits the tourists' hard currency and they have introduced the international practice of green lines (nothing to declare) and red lines (something to declare). Of course, Russians like the colour red so much that they closed all the green lines and forced us to go through the red lines.

We were met by Yury's assistant, Marianna Shub, a neatly dressed woman flashing a friendly smile and a pair of black eyes that give away nothing, and Igor Pogrebinski, a big man with a round, ruddy face wearing a Gestapo-style leather jacket and with a very pushy and abrasive manner. He shoved us into a battered yellow Lada taxi and we raced like fiends along the pot-holed highway to Moscow. Yury, apparently, was teaching that night and wouldn't be able to get together with me until the morning. He is working with the first-year students at the Moscow Art Theatre School and will continue to do so until they graduate, and then he'll take the whole class into the Pushkin as part of his company. This sounds like a brilliant way to rejuvenate one's own company while at the same time ensuring that the incoming students and the resident company have a symbiotic working method and aesthetic style.

We passed by the CSKA Stadium, the home of the Red Army hockey team. Igor is clearly a fan. He reeled off the names of the four Russian players who have just started playing in the NHL. "It's not the same any more," he moaned. "The best players are all in North America."

We headed straight for the Hotel Russia opposite the Kremlin, so huge it takes up an entire city block. It has a reputed four thousand rooms. It was built, so tourists are told, to house the delegates from the various republics for the vast Communist Party meetings and to impress them with the power and efficiency of the communist system. In reality, the hotel is a superannuated, elephantine version of something one might find in the Jane/Finch corridor in Toronto. Did the post-war architecture of Moscow once have an austere beauty to it as judged in a world ruled by pragmatism? To a westerner indoctrinated with the values of the '80s, with marketing the god, the buildings only seem to be the product of lazy thinking. As we drove through the streets of the city the schizophrenia of contemporary Russia was immediately visible. On the one hand are the inhabitants of the world of traditional values, the overweight women, the short-tempered salespeople and the elderly veterans proudly promenading with their military medals pinned to their lapels. More obnoxious is the other world of sleazy pimps and cheap thugs who stand outside the hotels where foreigners stay. With unctuous arrogance they offer to change money at the black market rate or pester you for any western items you might want to sell or, better yet, give them. They drive taxis but won't move unless they can sucker you into an exorbitant rate. They are called the "Mafia" by the average citizen of Moscow and are denounced by the Party as an example of the evils of capitalism. Can this country survive with these two contradictory worlds existing side by side? No wonder the old-fashioned Soviets look at foreigners with a mixture of jealousy, hatred, fear and admiration.

The Hotel Russia is large enough to warrant four separate entrances, one for each point of the compass, and one of those entrances is devoted entirely to registration. There was no line-up but the wait was endless. If money has no meaning (the Pushkin is paying for the accommodation in roubles) then who cares if two more foreigners get their rooms or not?

Since Yury wasn't available until the next day I decided to spend my first evening taking in one of the plays in repertory at the Pushkin. Before the show I was taken around backstage. The cyc is water-stained and I could easily see the stitches where it has been repeatedly mended, the fly ropes are blackened, frayed hemp that look precarious, and the black masking is dirty and ripped. Everyone looked tired and morose, and the place seemed empty. Off a creaky and warped horseshoe corridor are the many actors' dressing-rooms. Each actor of the company, it seems, has one to himself. A visit to the actors' buffet yielded greasy salami, a slice of dry bread and a cup of coffee. On the wall is a "No Smoking" sign, but everyone was puffing away. The western anti-smoking trend has obviously not hit Russia. I took a deep breath and blinked. I thought I had time-travelled back forty years. At the age of five I spent one year in a war-torn German town when my father was stationed there with the Canadian Army. Everything from the feel of the toilet paper, the consistency of the sugar in the coffee, to the smell of the air reminded me of post-war Germany.

The auditorium of the Pushkin is large, old-fashioned and unremarkable. There is a Soviet hammer and sickle over the proscenium and boxes on either side of the stage. Could one take advantage of this? Could Theseus's court look like this? Should Theseus, Hippolyta and the lovers be in the boxes for the play-within-the-play? The stage is high and even from my seat in the fourth row it felt far away. Do they have a forestage? Would they let us come out into the house? Will they build a rake for the play? Do they have enough technicians and the time to instal a rake during the change-overs to the play? This looks like an impoverished theatre. Will they have the money to accommodate all the things I will want?

I watched a group of very tired actors perform an obscure French comedy, and nodded off during the first act—a victim of the small seats, the eight-hour time difference and the boring theatre. I was a good head higher than any of the Russians around me and I opened my eyes to find an actress in full acting flight staring right at me. The actors, I was sure, knew who I was and there I was falling asleep on them. Not a great first impression.

As I fled at intermission I was more convinced that the design of the theatre itself would help enhance the world of traditional Russia that both the court and the mechanicals should embody. If Theseus relates to the audience as his subjects and we dress his attendants in Russian military uniforms we might be able to tie the stage and the audience together in a significant manner.

Monday, October 9, 1989

Hermia: But I beseech your Grace that I may know
  The worst that may befall me in this case,
  If I refuse to wed Demetrius.
Theseus: Either to die the death, or to abjure
  For ever the society of men. (Act I, scene i)

I woke up late. This jet lag gets harder to cope with as one gets older.

A two-hour meeting to take the artistic team at the theatre through the concept of the production. We met in Yury's office, sitting in red velvet chairs so soft and low to the ground you can't get out once you've sunk in. Is this Stalinist plush? A jungle of letters and plays spilled impressively over his desk, and a large colour TV and VCR thrust out from one corner of the room. A dramaturge and a few assistants hovered in the background. How was I to start? How was I to get them excited rather than frightened by the ideas? I want to take this play and root it firmly in the maelstrom of modern Russia. I want this play to be so relevant it could have been written tomorrow. I want the Russians to be struck dumb that an Elizabethan could have understood their modern *Zagadka* so well. How much of this do I confide?

Will they think I am being presumptuous? Will they be insulted? Will the concept be politically too cheeky? Will they dismiss my understanding of Russia as superficial? With all this bouncing around in my head I started.

The world of the court must connote power, order, the army, I said. It must suggest the world of contemporary Russia. When Theseus warns Hermia, in scene one, that unless she obeys her father she must "die the death," we must believe that this Theseus has killed before and will do so again. (Should Theseus remind us a little of Gorbachev? I don't mention this because it is probably a red herring.) The forest world must reek of contemporary western rock, I explained, punk decadence. The mechanicals should be a collection of recognizable Soviet craftsmen, and we will change the references in the text to relate to contemporary occupations. Each worker should speak with an accent from a different part of the Soviet Union.

"Does this mean you want the mechanicals to represent Russia?" asked Yury, catching on quickly.

"Nothing in Shakespeare is ever as simple as an equation," I replied. "If the mechanicals represent Russia it might be in a poetic sense but never as a specific metaphor. They must be distinct Soviet types with a believable aura of reality about them so when they touch objects on stage these objects become objects from the real world."

I asked if we could get some kind of vehicle for the mechanicals' entrance. I noticed a few eyebrows going up. I had arranged my director's book so that each page consisted of Shakespeare on the right side, the Russian translation on the left and in the middle a literal, word for word translation from the Russian back into the English, that Yanina had done for me. This was to help me follow the actors in the text (my Russian was rudimentary and self-taught) and also to locate places in the Russian version where the translation was inaccurate. I expressed a worry that too many of Shakespeare's double entendres were missing, and used the example of the name "Bottom." In English it has a now-obscure reference to his craft (weaving). It can mean the underside of an object, but can also refer to the depth of things, and of course it is a polite moniker for "arse" or "ass." And an ass is precisely what the character Bottom gets transformed into in the forest. Now try to make all those levels work in Russian. They all giggled when I smacked my ass to demonstrate the pun. The bawdy side of Shakespeare is something most European translations of the Bard tend to ignore or have been unconsciously blind to. One wonders if the cultured Europeans simply didn't want to admit that the world's greatest playwright could have stooped so low as to include so many sexual connotations in his works. Olga Shvedova, the theatre's dramaturge, expressed a willingness to work on some of the emendations of the Russian text.

But my real worry, the quality of the acting, I don't mention. What I saw last night was rank amateur, with no attempt to reach the audience. Is this a product of Russian theatre tradition? Stanislavsky taken to the extreme? Is it a product of the actors' having to juggle too many roles in too many plays and having lost interest and conviction? Or is this something deeper, a product of Russian history itself? Do they just distrust in principle any attempt to reach out and contact the audience? Why would this be?

On the whole Yury behaved quite wonderfully. He was relaxed and very much in control of his staff. There was no petty in-fighting or negativism going on. I wonder how Yury will maintain a sense of team-work and common goals while all around him his country is falling apart. What kind of standards will he be striving for as the chaos deepens? I must keep my eyes open. Mark Lamos, the Artistic Director of the Hartford Stage Company in Connecticut, had directed a production of O'Neill's *Desire Under the Elms* for the Pushkin last season. I had phoned him to ask him if he had any tips on how to work in Russia. "Play all the European power games," he advised. "If they don't give you what you want just threaten to walk." I know that Yury's drive to hire western directors is tinged with opportunism. With Lamos he was able to wangle an invitation for the Pushkin to perform at a theatre festival in Connecticut and Yury had also been invited to direct in Hartford. What does he expect from me? One can't condemn this kind of opportunism. Yury is trying to find additional money for his theatre, and his relationship to government officials is made a great deal easier if he has recognition from abroad. Does this sound like Canada?

In addition, it is impossible to make qualitative comparisons between theatre in Moscow and theatre in Toronto. What in one city is a source of great aesthetic pride can be totally irrelevant in the other city. It is also true that a mere fascination with another culture can influence our judgement. When the Maly Theatre from Leningrad brought what was a superficial and outdated play to Toronto in 1988 it was fêted, mainly because of our hunger for things Russian.

When I finished talking they told me I can't have a forestage because of fire regulations and because the technical crew wouldn't have the time to remove it for the next play in the repertoire. After the meeting I took another walk around the stage. The deck is so shoddy it will need resurfacing if we are to use roller-skates or a skateboard. The fly gallery looks like it will cave in at any moment. But there is a lot of space under the stage for trap doors and entrances and there is a permanent revolve. Can these assets be exploited?

When founded in 1914 the theatre was called the Kammerni, which comes from the German word that means "chamber." Between the wars the theatre gained the reputation of being one of the most innovative and exciting stages in Europe. Stanislavsky, Meyerhold and Tairov were the three great Russian directors of the period. In 1949 Stalin had Tairov removed from his position as Artistic Director of the Kammerni and the theatre was renamed the Pushkin Theatre. Yury is clearly trying to regain some of the kudos of bygone days. He has had the spacious lobbies repainted with colourful murals that are reproductions of some of the expressionistic costume designs from the theatre in its heyday. The depictions are done in bold primary colours very characteristic of Soviet art at its creative high point in the '20s before the iron grip of Stalinism stifled all individuality.

In the evening Sasha Sergievsky, a translator and writer, introduced me to a co-operative restaurant near the Pushkin. "Co-operative" means anything that is not State-run; it is the beginning of capitalism and in the official newspapers the ventures have been consistently getting bad press. Stories of shoot-outs and gangsterism are regular items and now every Muscovite will tell you that all co-op restaurants are run by Azerbeidjan crooks. The food is usually wonderful, but much too expensive for the average citizen. So these restaurants are patronized only by tourists or Soviets who are earning money on the black market. You can eat your food surrounded by a lot of sleazy individuals.

Sasha has just had a translation of Pinter's *The Caretaker* open in town, the first Pinter to be officially produced in Russia. Poor Russia, theatre here will now be catching up on a lot of "decadent" western plays that are finally permissible. What a lot of bad theatre there will be in the name of that catching up. We were joined at the co-op by Assia DeVreeze, the former librarian at the National Theatre School in Montreal, and a very dear friend. For several generations of actors in this country she is one of the legends of Canadian theatre. Born in Russia, she fled during WWII and eventually made it to Canada where she raised her three kids on her own while expanding the minds and souls of the hundreds of students who, for over nearly twenty-five years, have passed through the school. Holed up in the library like some great mother goddess of the Ranidae, she would attack the complacent middle-class minds of most of the students with the self-satisfied grin of a frog that has just swallowed a fly. She still keeps in touch with many of the students for whom she is a kind of emotional archive. She has come to visit her daughter, Tamara Galko, who is working at the Canadian Embassy. The reunion was joyous. I had wanted nothing so much as to be with Assia on her first visit back to Russia.

After dinner, a long cab ride took us to the Theatre Studio in the Yugozapanyi (Southwest) where we caught the première of Camus's *Caligula*. Located in a tiny basement of the apartment building where Sasha and his wife Tanya live, the Theatre Studio is one of the original Russian fringe theatres. Over the years it developed a decent reputation both in the city and abroad for its "anti-system" productions. We sat way up in a corner squashed under a steel beam and had to watch the performance sideways on. It was a scary, claustrophobic experience. They were making a parallel between Caligula and Stalin, and the staging was imaginative, the music and acting very energetic as well. But why bother bashing Stalin any more? Aren't the problems different now?

There are no public bars or coffee shops where you can go for a beer after the show so we all crowded into Sasha's kitchen for tons of food and vodka amidst clouds of cigarette smoke. Someone translated the latest joke about a Russian who gets an exit visa and finally goes to live in Paris. Every morning he goes to a café and asks the waiter for a coffee, a croissant and a copy of *Pravda*. Every day the waiter replies, "You can have a coffee, you can have a croissant, but I'm sorry, we don't have a *Pravda* newspaper." This goes on for a week. Finally the waiter gets furious.

"I told you that you can have the coffee and the croissant but we don't have the fucking *Pravda*."

"Oh, please," says the Russian, "could you repeat that one more time?"

Everyone I met is disillusioned with Gorbachev because nothing is getting any better for them. Sasha and Tanya (who is Jewish) have been granted exit visas and are hoping to emigrate to Canada. They are doing it for their two kids. "On our own we could exist here in Russia, but not our children." I tried to warn them that they will be driving cabs or waitressing and cleaning toilets, but they refuse to be discouraged. Though Toronto is one of the better places in the world to be at the moment, they have no idea how rough they are going to have it.[2]

Tuesday, October 10, 1989

Fairy: And I serve the Fairy Queen,
  To dew her orbs upon the green. (Act II, scene i)

A meeting with the designers. Valery Fomin is the resident set designer for the Pushkin and a well-known Russian theatre artist. He is a small, quiet, gentle man with a goatee. Once again I described the play's three worlds and how each must be clearly delineated in its own right. Shakespeare had no trouble juxtaposing the mythical Greece of Theseus with the contemporary world of the mechanicals and the magical world of the fairies. Nor should we. Valery asked for clarification of the court: "If we have the

[2] As of February 1991 they were still in an immigration camp in Rome waiting for Canadian visas.

military figures on the stage, won't the audience identify them with the present?" I tried to explain that the visuals of the court should mix the past and the present but suggest a fictional benevolent dictatorship sometime in the future. We need to underscore the textual references to the battle between Theseus and Hippolyta, and make it clear that he has just won something akin to a civil war and that the Amazons are his prisoners. The story on stage begins with Theseus's decision not to kill the prisoners but to marry the Queen of the enemy instead.

Valery nodded: "But we also want Theseus's court to relate to the forest. In Russia the forest is everywhere. It is in our soul."

Wow! This could be brilliant. If the columns from the palace could metamorphose in front of our eyes into the trees of the forest, we would convey Shakespeare's sense that the forest is the flip-side of our day selves. I've always assumed that in choosing the play's title Shakespeare was talking about the night of Midsummer Day (summer solstice), the longest day of the year when, in northern climes, it is very difficult to tell where day ends and night begins. They blend into one. The problem is that the play doesn't go directly from the court into the forest. In between we have the world of the mechanicals (Act One, scene two). For this scene I'd like the theatrical masking to be flown out to expose the back walls and the bareness of the stage. Ideally the actors should enter from one of the storage areas backstage in order to bring with them the feel of workshops and the reality of work. Again Valery nodded. When I started talking about the two levels of the Elizabethan stage and the need for ramps and rakes, he interjected, "But ... but ... but, this is a repertory theatre. Whatever we build we have to be able to take down in two hours." Mark Lamos's advice started echoing in my ears. Should I throw a fit and shout, "I'm not working under these shoddy conditions," and walk out of the room? I'm not sure I can summon the kind of cynicism needed to pull it off. I prefer to try to get them excited about the production and develop their commitment. In the middle of our conversation the costume designer, Ksenia Shemanovskaya, a large, beautiful Wagnerian goddess with a long braid down to her waist, walked in. She'd been summoned by the theatre but hadn't a clue as to what the project was going to be. Her face broke into a quizzical grin as I explained the potential for the costumes, particularly the sexuality of the forest world. Does this mean she is resisting the possibilities? We all agreed to meet again in two days when both Valery and Ksenia will bring in some preliminary ideas to bounce around.

The reaction to the project has been vacillating between "This is intriguing" and "Who the hell does he think he is?" I simply have to fire up their imagination and get them desperately wanting to do the production.

The afternoon was spent auditioning ten of the senior actors of the company individually. I sat them down and asked them to do a monologue from the part they were currently playing that they hated the most. They were dumbfounded. "You mean that I am being tested? This is just like theatre school." Realizing Yury had not had the courage to tell them I was auditioning them and realizing they felt I was attacking their status within the company, I politely pressed on. One of the ten actors refused but the rest were game and we managed to have some fun. I threw them little challenges just to see what they had inside. One did a comic stutter, another a ridiculous French accent and they all sang with pleasure. They were at one and the same time technically stunning and distanced, alienated from their own selves. It felt as if they were miles away, actually miles away *inside* themselves. Is it going to be possible to get them to use their own charm to find the parts? The lovers in the play can very quickly become boring if the roles are merely acted; the actors have to discover a genuine innocence in themselves. I'm glad to say that six of the ten actors are worth calling back for a closer look and it seems that management deliberately left another six or seven senior actors I was to see off the list. Is this Marianna manipulating me? (She was in charge of organizing the auditions.) I insisted I get to see them.

In the evening I watched another play from the Pushkin repertoire, Glowacki's *The Depths*. Glowacki is a Polish emigré playwright whose play *Hunting Cockroaches* was produced last season by the Canadian Stage. Why do all productions at the Pushkin feel the same? Is it because I don't understand the language? I searched in vain for the magical silver thread between the stage and the audience. I simply couldn't detect one. Is Russia itself in such emotional disharmony that no silver thread is possible?

The day ended at the *Dom Actiera*,[3] the official building of the Actors' Union on Gorky Street. It has offices, conference rooms and a restaurant open only to theatre workers. The only alcohol available tonight was a cheap brandy that tasted like the proverbial antifreeze. A brash and drunken film critic joined our table. He found out we are foreigners, immediately became our best friend and opened up about the future of Russia.

"There is going to be a military coup," he proclaimed. He has no

---

[3] House of the Actors.

family and so will weather it out rather than leave the country. He has started his own film production company which specializes in servicing all the western films being shot in Russia. He is, he said with an ironic giggle, a "co-operator."

"Nobody can get into this restaurant except people like me," he smiled with feigned outrage. "No actors can afford it. Only gangsters and co-operators are here. It is common to have to pay the maître d' up to three hundred roubles for a table in a restaurant like this. This country is going crazy." While waving to or hailing half the people at the surrounding tables he rattled on, "I have a friend who opened a co-operative restaurant and is clearing seventy thousand roubles a month but the only thing that there is to spend money on is food, so he goes to other co-operative restaurants and spends his money there."

Our film critic was happy that a new option for spending money had recently opened up: Bulgaria. He could now go there for his holidays and find other co-operators and pimps and the mafia all sunning themselves side by side on the beaches. How much of this was the antifreeze talking? I wondered. Is one segment of the population intent upon partying themselves into oblivion while history is being made around them?

Wednesday, October 11, 1989

Oberon: Sound, music! Come, my queen, take hands with me,
   And rock the ground whereon these sleepers be. (Act IV, scene i)

A three-hour meeting on the music. Olga Abramenkova is the director of music for the Pushkin. A proper, direct woman, she brought in three pages of precise questions about the music. She also explained she had bumped into Arkady Serper, one of the best-known composers of theatre music in Moscow. He just happened to have completed the score for a production of *A Midsummer Night's Dream* in Muldavia. Just before he was due to go down there, however, ethnic unrest flared up and the theatre decided it might be better to hire a local composer. He was now wandering the streets of Moscow with an unused jazz score composed for the play. We sent for him.

Within half an hour a small, nervous man in faded clothes and with a slight stoop arrived. I plunged in and went through the play page by page, detailing the position and function of the music cues. I explained that Theseus's court needs an anthem that resembles and is possibly even a take-off of the Soviet national anthem.

"Should it be a funny parody?" asks Arkady.

"It should be able to surround the Duke with an aura of military power," I reply. The lovers need a love theme that works on a single instrument, but can also be fleshed out with more instruments for larger moments in the play. We also need a death theme to underscore the constant references to dying. It would be ideal, I suggested, if the love theme and the death theme in some way used many of the same notes but to a different effect. Perhaps one is the reverse of the other. Thus, love and death can be inextricably intertwined. And I insisted that the mechanicals should be able to play some imitation Russian folk music live. Olga quickly interjected that she can get any of the actors playing any instrument in six months. (She is probably quite strict. I wouldn't want to be in her hands.) I proposed that the mechanicals' theme song be the one Bottom sings in Act Three, scene one, to Titania, "The Ousel Cock." Arkady didn't know what I was talking about. A quick comparison of our texts revealed that Bottom's song and many other references to the music are inexplicably missing. What kind of Shakespeare have the Russians been doing for the last sixty years?[4]

Arkady got very excited when I mentioned I wanted the music in the forest to be heavy metal. "Heavy metal!" he shouted, bouncing off his chair. "What kind? Def Leppard, Led Zeppelin, Iron Maiden? I've got all of them."

As an artist from the decadent west, I didn't dare let on that I couldn't tell these groups apart. We agreed to meet on Saturday to choose some suitable music. Arkady was visibly sagging under the number of cues I had given him, though pretending otherwise, so we didn't get through the whole text. I assured him I was merely giving suggestions and of course he was free to add and develop his own ideas for the piece. I feel I have a composer who loves the concept for the show and who will rise to the occasion. In this dusty Russian theatre I have an ally. Instruments will be a problem, though. They have no electric violins to support the music of Titania and her followers, and there is no available equipment for the rock

[4] Arkady's version was published in the thirties. We discovered chunks of text that had been edited. For instance, Puck never got to undo the magic on Lysander's eyes in Act Four. I'd love to concoct some theory of Stalinist censorship but I think it was simply the modern version of a "compositor's error." The original translation published in the twenties had no missing lines or stage directions.

band that should back up Oberon: no electric guitars, no synthesizers, no echo machines, no amplifiers.

Throughout the various meetings of the past few days Andrey Shiriayev, assigned to the production as the assistant director, sat silently in a corner making notes in a tiny notebook. Tall, fiftyish, with the dignified servility of a Prussian butler, he is the kind of professional assistant director, I suspect, who is supportive, but too timid to exhibit any initiative of his own.

In the afternoon the rest of the older male actors read for the parts of the mechanicals. The first was quite bitter. He had been with the theatre long before Yury took over as Artistic Director four years ago. As a member of the old guard he was now out of favour. He couldn't be fired because Soviet actors are employed by theatres for life, so instead he was simply ignored. He sat there glumly. Is this a Quince? A possessive, pedantic, kind old man? I gave him one of Quince's speeches and he read it rather well. When asked to improvise a carpenter who has come to fix the door to the audition room while taking furtive nips from a bottle in his back pocket, he made a rather feeble effort, though the secret drinking was very convincing. On the whole these actors are neither driven by a hungry egotism, nor striving to achieve a set of standards. They are dulled by the lack of any challenges. Two possible nuggets have been sifted out, however. One has a sex appeal that will serve Oberon well and the other, tight-lipped and barrel-chested, might be a Theseus.[5]

A female actor barged into the auditions asking to be seen as she couldn't make the scheduled times for the women. I asked her if she had a monologue in the repertoire she hated.

"No," she replied.

I asked her if she had any monologue she could deliver.

"No," she replied.

I asked her if she could sing a song. She sang a cappella for about two seconds. I asked her if she was prepared to improvise.

"No," she replied.

By now I'm pissed off. I thanked her and waved her out of the room. At this point I noticed what I thought was my change purse on the table so I swept it up and put it in my pocket.

She stared at me in amazement, and turned to the assistant director as he was dismissing her and blurted, "But he took my wallet!"

I pulled her change purse out of my pocket and then took out my own, one I had bought in Moscow on a previous visit. They were identical.

[5] Alexander Yermakov and Valery Barinov, respectively. Both ended up with the roles.

We both had a good laugh. I wonder if the actors will start to think that I take bribes.

Should I be bringing over the Michel St. Denis masks from the National Theatre School? Some mask work might help the Russians find the centre of their emotions and transcend the introverted technicality of their acting style.

Tonight the theatre arranged for us to eat in the restaurant of the Dom Kino, the official building of the film workers' union. An artistic director from a theatre in Riga tried to chat me up, desperately seeking an invitation for his company to come to Toronto. The lure of and need for hard currency has Soviet theatre directors working overtime trying to get west.

Thursday, October 12, 1989

Demetrius: No remedy, my lord, when walls are so
  willful to hear without warning. (Act V, scene i)

Valery has been busy. For our second session he brought in a rough model with all sorts of interesting bits of shiny plastic and hanging threads. He also had a collection of pictures, some of which spoke to me, and we agreed they would serve as further inspiration. I liked a series of Ionic columns that looked like the columns in the theatre's auditorium, and a fractured image of a human face distorted as if through mirrors. "Yes, it would work if in the forest the images of the lovers ended up at times looking like this," I commented. The model also had a raked floor and ramps.

"What we could do," Valery said, "is make the columns out of a polyethylene vinyl of some kind so we can inflate them. We'd start with an empty stage and then from nothing the columns pop up. Then we pull the columns into the air and the feet have roots and mirrors and shiny things attached to them. This becomes the forest." A fabulous concept! The upstage ramp can be suspended between two line sets so there will be no need for any supporting structure to clutter up the stage. When we want to bring on the mechanicals we just fly out the masking and the borders, and we can see the whole backstage area, even catch some of the technicians at work in the wings. We can throw on a bright work light and presto! We have a real world for the mechanicals to play their first scene in.

We discussed the vehicle the mechanicals will use for their entrance. First a baggage cart was suggested, but it was pointed out it would be too heavy for the stage to bear. Then Valery mentioned a kind of invalid's vehicle unique to Russia that looks like a motorized sardine can. I've seen them in the streets and liked the idea immediately. The mechanicals are, of course, the clowns of the play and this vehicle might have a peculiarity to it that could help us. They think it might go at least half-way up the raked stage. We've started, I thought. Valery is game. But how are we going to finance it? Valery said that is not his problem. We agreed we would have to have something more precise by Monday.

In the afternoon it was time to try to find a Titania. The female star of the Oscar-winning *Moscow Without Tears* is a lovely actress but too old and too "tasteful" for the part. Another dumpy but vibrant woman has a great sense of humour and might just work as one of the mechanicals. Could she play Quince? I've seen the part played by a woman but I worry about encroaching upon the macho locker-room atmosphere that is useful as part of the "boys' world." Another actor stormed out of the room because I laughed at what I thought was a very funny delivery of a speech and she thought I was laughing at her. My audition methods are apparently a source of much gossip throughout the theatre. So far only one actor had the initiative to get hold of the play and read it before the audition. Everyone else had only heard about the plot or done bits of the play at theatre school. If these actors were forced to survive in New York they would starve to death for lack of initiative.

Tonight Assia's daughter, Tamara Galko, the Cultural Attaché at the Canadian Embassy, threw a party for a cross-section of theatre artists in the city. Assia has been following the auditions with glee, even taking pictures of the actors with a tiny camera in the middle of their audition pieces. She has a natural and honest gregariousness about her and everyone has taken to her immediately. When Anatoly Vassiliev's company took Pirandello's *Six Characters in Search of an Author* to the Féstival des Amériques in Montreal last summer, the entire cast somehow found their way to the most Russian piece of real estate in the whole city, Assia's kitchen, where they spent all their evenings drinking, eating, smoking and talking. Tonight these actors had a joyful reunion with her. Ksenia was also there. I'd located a copy of a video of *Mad Max Beyond the Thunderdome* so we turned it on to give her some ideas for the costumes. All the Russians immediately collected in front of the VCR, struck dumb by this example of western art.

It is not the usual practice for Canadian Embassy officials to entertain the "natives" in their diplomatic quarters. This is no doubt some faded remnant of an External Affairs department trying to be very correct and "British," but Tamara is able to do her job more efficiently precisely because she knows the people so well. We all assumed that the apartment is bugged and that the walls have ears, so we made a few toasts to the KGB listening.

Friday, October 13, 1989

Bottom: ... my chief humour is for a tyrant. I could play Ercles rarely,
   (Act I, scene ii)

At lunch a cousin of Yanina's, an architect with a project in Muldavia, talked about the situation in that increasingly tense southern republic. The Muldavians recently passed a law forbidding the use of Russian in any official capacity. (Their Bill 101?) The Muldavians, after years of being under the yoke of Moscow, are trying, like the Baltic Republics, to establish some independence. How far will it go? No one knows, the cousin said. He suspects people will compromise with a solution that will satisfy no one.

After lunch, back at the Pushkin, Yury was rehearsing a Dostoevsky play. I sneaked into the director's box and watched the proceedings for a while. The director's box is not accessible from the lobby, only from the office of the artistic director. It has a curtain that can be drawn so the actors are never sure if someone is inside watching them. The rehearsal itself is astonishing. Yury, with single-minded fanaticism, bullies the actors into doing exactly as he wants. They change their blocking or delivery with silent acquiescence while Yury jumps up and down in his seat, runs on the stage with his arms waving and sometimes even screams at them face to face.[6] This is a working method few actors in the English-speaking theatre would accept. No chance here for the actor's intelligence to be part of the creative process. (True, Yury did seem to treat the more senior actors with

---

[6] Back in Canada in the spring of 1990 the CBC aired Ken Dryden's hockey series on TV. In the episode on Soviet hockey the camera caught the Soviet coach in the middle of a game shouting nose to nose at some of his players. This is obviously an accepted pattern of behaviour in the Soviet Union. The results, in hockey anyway, are certainly impressive.

a modicum of respect.) Is this why the atmosphere on stage is so introverted? Why so little is given to the audience?

I sneaked out of the box shaking my head and then started five hours
of call-backs. With the mechanicals I again risked impropriety and asked all
the actors to come into the room together. Switching parts around rapidly,
I had them improvise a song while playing imaginary musical instruments.
Then we had various stabs at Act One, scene two. Two actors stand out.
One is big and gangly with a great smile and a lovely sense of humour. He
might make a perfect chauvinist, slightly slow Bottom. The best actor of
the lot would make a great Flute. Flute ends up playing Thisby in the play
before the court and the death of Thisby is, to my mind, one of the most
difficult acting tasks in the whole play. Nina Marushina, the dumpy, funny
female actor, could be a good risk for Starveling. She is round and anything
but starving so perhaps she can be continually eating to earn her ironic
nickname. Quince might be a tiny, bespectacled, older actor. The struggle
between Quince and Bottom will thus end up as a struggle between big
and little.

For Hermia I settled on a cute, dark, young girl who is more vulnerable than I have ever imagined Hermia played. The actress actually blushes
at some of the lines. A young, good-looking and self-conscious student
from the graduating class of the Moscow Art Theatre School will make a
good Lysander. The character is Shakespeare's tongue-in-cheek picture of
poets as lovers. For Demetrius I decided on a big, funny actor, very
handsome in a burly Russian way. But casting Helena is a problem. Do I
go with the tall, lithe beauty, who went so far as to learn one of the
monologues for her audition, or do I go with the more good-natured
blonde with the great singing voice? The blonde, Irina Biakova, has the
rare ability to allow outsiders to enter into her soul as she acts, and the
character of Helena is one of Shakespeare's "Fortune's fools," who needs
to make an open and real contact with the audience. Titania will be Maria
Zubareva. This last bit of casting is by default and one of the risks for the
production.

Ksenia has with breath-taking speed whipped up some costume sketches
for us to talk about. What an original imagination! She has played around
with a mixture of leather and veils for the lovers that can only be described
as fairy tale punk. Puck could be out of a *Mad Max* sequel. I'm thrilled!
But how will we continue the director-designer dialogue once I am gone?
Will the Canadian Embassy let us FAX drawings back and forth? And how
is the theatre going to finance these costumes?

It's nearly two a.m. Yuri, a painter friend of Ksenia's with a Viking-red beard, has just driven me home from her apartment, where she fed us and showed us her paintings. Ksenia considers herself to be a painter first and a costume designer only in her spare time. One haunting canvas was of her own grandmother sitting in a rocking chair and staring out at the world with a puzzled, pained look. This woman was an original member of the Communist Party and a devoted revolutionary all her life. Her prize possession as she grew old was a document attesting to her contribution to the Revolution. One day she lost it. She was literally struck dumb, and spent the last four years of her life silently rocking in her chair, locked in a world inside her head. Ksenia captured this look with eerie sympathy. Where are these committed communists today?

Saturday, October 14, 1989

Bottom: This is Ercles' vein, a tyrant's vein; (Act I, scene ii)

Late Saturday evening. Each day wipes out the memory of the one before. What happened yesterday? I can't remember. Moscow is a cocoon that isolates one from the rest of the world. Now that's Toronto-centricity for you! Every morning I wake up and have to figure out what I am doing here all over again. Have I been away a month? A year?

Assia told me she heard that I won't get the set I want, that the theatre doesn't have the facilities to provide the necessary technical elements and that they can't afford the production. Hmm ...

Yury Yeremin has recommended Oleg Kiselev as the movement coach. He is the director of a small troupe who has developed a unique brand of movement theatre he calls "contact improvisation," which encompasses everything from dance through mime to an off-the-wall use of verbal experimentation. He had demonstrated his work at the Stanislavsky conference in February. Oleg takes his actors' bodies and himself beyond the bounds of what most western movement teachers would deem physically permissible. I am sure he would argue that he understands the body better than western movement experts do. I went along to the miniscule basement apartment he and his artists use as their headquarters and rehearsal studio. In a room with a very low ceiling and hardly larger than a tool shed, in which the actors pretend to have twenty times as much space as they actually do, Oleg gave us a true demonstration of tyranny. Bellowing at the actors with his fist raised was his preferred method to get them to "act better." But those actors have developed an elasticity with their bodies far beyond anything I've ever seen.[7]

The one part that can not be cast adequately from the resident company at the Pushkin is Puck. And Puck is too important to the production to allow a false sense of propriety force me into miscasting the part. The whole show would suffer. Without telling anyone at the theatre, I had arranged to meet an actor by the name of Sergei Agapitov in Oleg's studio. I'd seen him act in an adaptation of Strindberg's *Miss Julie* in a converted community centre in February. He arrived, in the usual Russian manner, an hour later than agreed, admitting he'd never read *A Midsummer Night's Dream* but shrugging that of course he knew the story. He read some of Puck's lines hesitantly, looking up for affirmation after every few words. This midget of a man, with hair that stands on end and bloodshot eyes peering out of a face that looks like a dried apple, was a circus performer, not a trained actor at all. He could be a Puck to end all Pucks. I had to have him. I told him I would speak to the Pushkin and have them hire him. Little lights seemed to flare up in his eyes. Was he trying to hide his enthusiasm or was he frightened?

Oleg returned to the Pushkin with me to talk about movement and to meet the composer. I told him I thought I needed both a choreographer and a fight director.

"What do you want a choreographer for?" he asked. "These aren't dancers. They can't do a break-dance, only an imitation of one. And if you want them to do an erotic *pas de deux* the actors must improvise it so that they can handle it with conviction."

If he can pull this off I am ready to go this route. He wants to start working with the actors right away to get them into shape. And Arkady and Olga want to start the actors off on the music and the instruments right away as well. This means they will have five months of preparation before I arrive in April for rehearsals. Naturally, this makes me a little paranoid. I'll be half-way around the world. How do I keep in touch?

---

[7] Oleg and his company have twice been to the Edmonton Fringe, most recently during the summer of 1990. He and some of his troupe decided to stay and try to make a go of it in Canada. When they first arrived they found their way (where else?) to Assia's in Montreal. She ended up having to pay bus fare to Edmonton for two members of the group so they could perform.

Arkady played some new music. The mechanicals' theme is perfect: folksy, a little romantic, humorous and moving. Altogether very Russian. The anthem for Theseus's court is also humorous and that is a mistake. He agreed to rewrite it. He will put all the music on a cassette and send it to Canada for my comments.

Sunday, October 15, 1989

Bottom: First, good Peter Quince, say what the play treats on; then read the names of the actors; and so grow to a point. (Act I, scene ii)

I spent the morning as a tourist. First to Zagorsk, forty miles outside Moscow, the holiest place in all of Russia. A hilltop of golden cupolas and church spires surrounded by ancient white walls, the monastery of Zagorsk makes a quintessential calendar photo. The courtyards were packed with eager Russians enjoying the new (if still unofficial) acceptance of the Orthodox Church. Most seemed dazed as they wandered around the courtyards, staring at the magnificent ecclesiastical architecture. A gaggle of KGB officers was there on an outing. What was that look in their eyes? Are they embarrassed to be seen enjoying religious buildings under the curious gaze of westerners? Every now and then you could spot the flowing black robes of the bearded Orthodox priests as they pushed their way through the crowds with the self-conscious sense of purpose of children on a parents' day at school. I found the atmosphere of the masses desperately thronging for some spiritual sustenance very disturbing, and blocked out as much as I could by listening to Pink Floyd's "The Wall" on a Walkman.

We sped back down the highway to another "must-do" tourist trap, the huge flea market at Ismailova. Driving in Moscow has special perils for foreigners. There are few, if any, maps, and those there are can be very misleading. One is told this is a deliberate attempt to fool the enemy in case of invasion. Obviously the Russians know American satellites have photographed every inch of the city so this explanation is interesting for what it says about the attitude of Russians towards tourists. It is true, though, that the possibility of a foreign invasion has been part of the daily mental diet of Soviet life since the Revolution. Along the highway at all the major intersections traffic police sit in glass-encased observation booths. As our state-of-the-art Mercedes Benz with its diplomatic plates zips by, the police pick up a phone and report on our progress to some communication centre. Every diplomat lives with the assumption that his or her vehicle is fixed up with, at the very least, some electronic bug that permits the KGB to track the location of the car. What an extraordinary waste of bureaucratic manpower.

There was little of much value and much of little value at the flea market. Also some very obscene-looking barbecued kebabs. We were warned that the consequence of this timid foray into a market economy is petty crime and to keep our hands on our wallets at all times.

In the late afternoon, back at the theatre, the actors were summoned to a company meeting. I asked Yury to read out the casting so I could carefully watch the reactions. Oleg Antonov's face broke into a huge grin when he heard he had got the part of Bottom, and the girls playing Helena and Hermia jumped out of their seats with joy and hugged each other. Two were sour-faced: Elena Skorokhodova, who wanted to play Helena and has ended up with the role of Hippolyta,[8] and Vadim Ledogorov, who was hurt that he was asked to play what he saw as the insignificant part of Flute/Thisby. I decided I had to catch him after the meeting to explain privately the importance of Thisby's function of turning the comedy around into a tragedy.

Then I elaborated on "what the play treats on," the shorter version. I stressed that although the visual elements would be modern we would be fanatical in our respect for Shakespeare's text. I asked them to get a copy of the play and to read it once together but not to learn any of the lines because I would like these to come only as we journeyed together to a better understanding of the play. I asked for questions. There was total silence. Why? Had Yury set such a formal tone to the proceedings that they were too inhibited to speak up? Maybe they didn't care for the play, the concept, the director? Do Russians have no sense of participatory creativity? What is going on here? A huge black cloud of doom and gloom moved in to hover over my head. Can I pull this off?

Afterwards in his office I explained to Yury why I had asked him not to announce any casting for the part of Puck. I tried to impress on him how important the role is to the play and the concept for the show, and begged his indulgence to go outside his company for the actor I wanted. The part needed danger, it needed darkness, it needed humour. I needed Sergei Agapitov. After barely a pause Yury responded that he didn't know the

---

[8] In December 1990, after opening, Elena got to play Helena. See Appendix C.

actor in question but if Sergei were prepared to work for five roubles a day on contract and not demand to become part of the permanent company, then he would see what he could do. He looked at me with that eager, driven smile of his and I couldn't tell if I was getting the straight goods or not. Did he sense that this was one issue over which I was absolutely prepared to walk? Was he retreating tactically until the Russian winter set in and he could attack my lines of communication?

Monday, October 16, 1989

Theseus: "The thrice three Muses mourning for the death
  Of Learning, late deceas'd in beggary." (Act V, scene i)

On my final day of this visit to Moscow the realities of Soviet theatre came crashing down on me. Among the seven hours of meetings spent trying to get as far as possible with discussions about designs for the set and costumes, and to set up lines of communication between Toronto and Moscow, was the key meeting with the Direktor (General Manager) of the Pushkin. Orlov is a soft-spoken man who chain-smokes and leans forward solicitously as he talks. He gave a brief biography of himself, stating that he is one of the most experienced and successful managers in Russian theatre and that he has worked anywhere worth working. OK. OK. What was he getting at? Then it comes: "The production will cost in my estimate about eighty thousand roubles and that is our entire budget for two years for new shows. We can't afford the set and costumes as they are. We will have to postpone the opening for one year." Basta! Just as I was getting a little taste of what it might be like to work with the actors, just as my director's electrons were starting to get excited, he suggests we postpone for one year. Not possible!

Originally we had agreed on May rehearsals and an early June opening because this was the only time my personal schedule would allow me to come back to Moscow. I was not sure, given the state of the Canadian Stage, when there might next be another opportunity. Besides, what was my guarantee that the theatre would not choose to postpone the show again? So I insisted we continue to aim for a June opening and the actors were to know nothing about a possible delay. I was desperately afraid they would lose their drive if they suddenly had no deadline. Orlov agreed.

Then quietly, careful not to offend me, and perhaps with a certain embarrassment, he asked whether I thought I might be able to get a Canadian company of some kind to sponsor the production. I dismissed the idea curtly, declaring that no Canadian corporation would be interested in the idea. The Direktor retreated. "I understand, of course," he murmured. I realized then that this meeting was the culmination of a week's clever manoeuvring. These crafty Russians! I had been set up. They knew how much I wanted this. I began mentally to try to rearrange my schedule to accommodate an additional visit to Moscow in one year's time.

Will I have a set, though, even in the fall? Yury, who tactfully left the room while Orlov broached the subject of a Canadian sponsor, now came back in and told a hair-raising story of an opening the previous night of a Théâtre du Soleil production from Paris that is visiting the Sovremennik Theatre here in town. He had phoned for tickets only to find out that the set had never been built. The materials had just never been delivered. They had been left to rot in the rain on some quay-side along the river. Russia, this great *Zagadka!* My *Zagadka* is, "Will I have a set?"

FIRST INTERMISSION

November to March flew by and Moscow became for a while just another city in the newspaper headlines to be sipped down with the morning coffee. While Europe was continuing its metamorphosis out of a post-war mind-set, the Berlin wall tumbling down and Russia still wrestling with the last vestiges of its Stalinist legacy, I was fighting my own battles at the Canadian Stage. Trying to put together a new season and a budget with a General Manager who neither understood my work nor was prepared to support it was a humiliating experience. More and more the executive of the board was pitting the General Manager against me in the time-honoured strategy of divide and conquer, while with the zeal of dilettantes they meddled in the running of the company and so made the situation among the staff worse every day.

Our culture has such fear of the creative process and so little respect for artists that the management consultants and marketing experts have to pretend in front of all the other corporate board members that they know how to run an artistic organization. One particularly imaginative member of the executive, the head of an advertising firm, was insisting we stop producing new, innovative work in the two small theatres in order to focus on shows that made money in the large theatre. This is about the same as telling an oil exploration firm to drill for brine because it is cheaper. The Canadian Stage Company was founded to develop and promote exciting Canadian work. In theatre there is no such thing as a safe commercial bet. A quick look at the most financially successful shows in London or New York will reveal that they are also the new shows. Theatre by its very nature is a risk, and if you don't like risks don't do theatre. This, however, is Canada and we don't think for ourselves. The greatest irony is that the President of the board of the Canadian Stage, while pretending to lead the organization with his superior financial skills, had seen the shares of his own company plummet and lose one hundred million dollars in value on the stock exchange.

In the end I put together a season intended to clearly define the mandate of the company for the artists, the granting agencies and, most importantly, the theatre-going public. It contained a mix of large and small productions, safe ones and risks. I felt secure that enough of the risks would prove winners to offset those that didn't succeed. I often wondered what Yury would say about how we run our theatres in Canada.

I sent a skateboard for Puck back to Moscow with a group of Russians who had been on a visit to Toronto. Was he practising? How were the music and the movement sessions progressing? Ksenia sent some sketches through the Canadian Embassy and they were so exciting, so appropriate, they made the hair on my head stand on end. After ruminating over the idea of a Canadian sponsor for the production, I accepted that it might be a fabulous opportunity for some corporation to gain a little presence in Russia while the Pushkin got some serious financial support. My first thought was to see if Labatt's Breweries was interested, as they have a long and very committed relationship to the development of new Canadian work. The prospect of two hundred and fifty million thirsty Soviets might get a brewery interested in some exposure in the lobby of a major cultural institution. No luck. After the idea was thrown around the marketing offices at Labatt's the word came back that they were not interested at the moment.

One hundred yards from the theatre, on Pushkin Square, McDonald's Canada had obtained permission to build the first Big Mac outlet in the Soviet Union. I suspected that they and Coca-Cola, their partner in the venture, might be interested in a sponsorship but in the past both companies had had an inconsistent and patronizing relationship with Canadian Stage and I did not want to squander this "golden" opportunity on businesses that didn't deserve it. Then, while in Ottawa working at the National Arts Centre on a production about the Avro Arrow, I met Gregg MacDonald, the Chairman of the ECS Group of Companies, which is involved in setting up a joint venture with the Soviets to develop Arctic navigational systems. Gregg is a wiry, somewhat acerbic and old-fashioned entrepreneur with sufficient imagination to realize the benefits of sponsoring the show. In fact, he jumped at the idea.

As the date of my return to Moscow approached, things settled down a little at the Canadian Stage. At a meeting with a committee the board had set up to ensure the artistic continuity of the theatre, I outlined my plans for the future, which included a repertory company producing a wide range of plays in four spaces. Everyone smiled profusely and was very encouraging. They also seemed to understand that it was not enough to replace the General Manager and that the relationship between the administration and the art had to be clearly defined in order to get rid of the chaos in the organization. We had had a good season, though not a banner one; the operating loss was heading toward being the smallest in the last five years. We had succeeded in taking the theatre back on the road to some kind of artistic consistency while hinting at the possibilities of what was yet to come. As I was getting ready to leave for Moscow, however, I heard but didn't take notice of a very distant tinkling of alarm bells in the corridors of my mind.

Five days before I was due to leave to start rehearsing, I received a phone call from London, England—the Half Moon Theatre was having a memorial service for Maurice Colbourne and would I like to participate? Maurice and I had co-founded the Half Moon in the early '70s. He was a big, slow-moving Yorkshire man with enormous integrity and an amiable charm as an actor who had been rewarded with a modest stardom as a lead in one of England's longest running television series, "Howard's End." He had died of a heart attack in the fall of 1989 when only in his forties. He had simply keeled over into the arms of his wife after repairing the roof of their newly acquired summer home in Brittany.

The early '70s in England was an era when the energy and creativity of an entire generation translated into the founding of hundreds of small theatres and theatre troupes around the country. Having graduated from McGill, I decided that if I was going to work in theatre, then I had better learn my craft, and so I set out on a wandering apprenticeship in Europe. I arrived in London from Berlin, where I had worked as an assistant director at the Schiller Theatre. Since I was not able to get a job in an established theatre (mainly because of my colonial accent) I had to start a theatre of my own. Somehow I met up with Maurice, who was living in a disused synagogue in the East End, and together we rolled up our sleeves and converted the synagogue into a theatre. By the time I returned to Canada in 1976, the Half Moon had become one of the most successful and highly subsidized small theatres in England. Later, with the help of the local

Borough Council, it acquired larger premises. By the late '80s Thatcherism had all but wiped out the prolific small theatre culture of the '70s. Now the Half Moon was also facing the prospect of having its British Arts Council grant cut. The memorial service was planned as a fund-raiser to help the cash-strapped theatre.

The evening was also a tribute to the memory of Jack Dash, one of the East End's most revered docker leaders. That an actor and a docker should be honoured on the same evening was a testament to the original aspirations of the Half Moon. We had been determined to develop a professional company of the highest standards that was of and for the East End community. Those early years of working side by side with Maurice were straight out of a working-class Andy Hardy plot. At the start there was little money so the actors worked for a cut of the box office. The materials for the first sets were scrounged from local building sites and condemned buildings. Any ready cash we had came from ripping off lead from the roofs of warehouses that were being demolished in our area. (The spot price for lead at the time at the local scrap metal dealers was sixty-five shillings a hundredweight.) We recruited a board of directors for the theatre that was exclusively made up of members of the community, such as dockers and construction workers. If we needed something I would just phone one of them: "Mick, the set for the next show calls for fifteen sheets of plywood."

"Come on down to the site at noon. The foreman will be off."

I would back the theatre van onto the construction site where Mick was working and while one member of his crew would climb up the scaffolding to keep a look-out, the rest would quickly fill the vehicle with building materials. Then I'd drive around the corner, lock up and buy the men a round of drinks in the local pub. That was how we did business in the East End.

This memorial evening at the Half Moon, attended by actors, playwrights, local kids with fabulously coloured spiky hair-dos and dockers dressed meticulously in suits, was a lovely blend of music, comic routines and reminiscences of Maurice and Jack. I tried to paint a picture of my ex-partner as I had known him in the early '70s: a rambling, lovably absentminded actor fresh out of theatre school. His girlfriend at the time owned a battered VW Beetle with a sun-roof through which we stuffed the lumber for the renovations to the synagogue that we'd scavenged from the nearby demolition sites. Maurice had never bothered to get a driver's licence and around the corner from the theatre was a police station. With sixteen-foot floor joists sticking through the roof of the Bug we would wave cavalierly to the "Nick" as we drove by. We had a plumber hook up the heating in the building and by-pass the gas meter. For four years we heated the place and never paid a penny. Just as I was leaving the country British Gas was digging up the street in front of the theatre. When I asked one of the workers what they were doing he replied they were somehow losing a lot of gas in the area and they were looking for leaks. Maurice by this time had landed a lead in a Walt Disney film and was being picked up every day in a limousine from the ramshackle house, a former brothel condemned by the local authorities, where he was squatting. Among many roles at the Half Moon he had played a very creditable Falstaff in a confused production of *Henry IV* I had directed, so I read a few of Falstaff's lines for him and hoped that he could hear. Afterwards when I was standing alone in the crush at the bar nursing a beer, dejected because I didn't feel I had done his memory justice, a docker I didn't know came up and shook my hand. "That was the finest tribute I've ever heard," he said. Later Maurice's wife, whom he had met only after he left the Half Moon, told me, "I never knew that Maurice."

A cloud of gloom hung over the evening, thanks to the poll tax riot in Trafalgar Square that afternoon. What started as a peaceful march by a quarter of a million people turned into the most horrific violence I've ever witnessed. The police tried to break up the crowds by backing their vans indiscriminately into the demonstrators, who retaliated by scaling scaffolding in front of a building overlooking the Square and pelting the police with any hard object they could get their hands on. I left my friends and pushed my way out of the Square just as the mounted riot squads were arriving and the crowds were trying to firebomb the South African High Commission. Heading up Charing Cross Road, I took one last look back. There on top of Canada House was our red maple leaf waving serenely over the chaos. It was a long way from the early '70s to the late '80s. Now violence, poverty, hatred and thousands of homeless people living in cardboard boxes under Waterloo Bridge had become acceptable and normal. Thatcher's England had lost the ability to be outraged by itself.

SECOND PERIOD

Rehearsals, April 1990

Sunday, April 1, 1990

Puck: Lord, what fools these mortals be! (Act III, scene ii)

Back in Moscow on April Fools' Day. Who is fooling who here? Customs and Immigration went quickly. Should one be judging the changes in the USSR by the increased efficiency at the airport?

There was Marianna in the throng of people awaiting arrivals. As always her appearance was studied: neat hair-do, western-style clothing and an indecipherable smile. The theatre has hired a car from the State car pool for my stay. It is a beaten-up, dirty old Lada, and the driver is a sullen, emaciated Soviet with rounded shoulders that give him an ingratiating air. He follows my every move with watchful brown eyes. One of the theatre's administrators has been sent on holiday to the Black Sea so that I can stay in his apartment. This arrangement is cheaper than putting me up in a hotel.

The city is soggy with melted snow and the streets are caked with mud accumulated from a winter of sanding. Moscow is dirtier and drearier than I remembered it, even after London. The apartment is on the outskirts of town in a typical post-war block high-rise, one of a seemingly endless number of similar blocks, separated by a few trees and winding paths. "Don't walk around alone at night," Marianna said, explaining that the administrator who lived here had recently been knifed by a gang of teenagers. She showed me how to make the double set of double-locked doors work and then proudly displayed some chicken on the stove which she had taken pains to cook. "It is getting more difficult to buy food," she remarked. As she put the lid back on the pan a couple of cockroaches scurried into hiding. How is this vulnerable country going to defend itself against the invasion of western culture? I'm glad to be back in Moscow and can't wait to get to work.

Monday, April 2, 1990

Oberon: And each several chamber bless,
  Through this palace, with sweet peace, (Act V, scene i)

Through Tamara Galko I had learned, while still in Canada, that the movement coach, Oleg Kiselev, had not had a good time at the Pushkin. Oleg had walked off the production, stating that the actors were not interested in imaginative, creative work, that the Pushkin had a poor reputation in the city and that I should take the production elsewhere. It was the day off at the theatre so I couldn't start rehearsals, but the entire production staff, the music and design team, awaited me with eager faces. They were all packed into Orlov's office, press-ganged by Yury to counter any of Oleg's accusations about the Pushkin perhaps not being behind this project and to paper over the cracks in Soviet artistic solidarity. Yury has invested a great deal of his theatre's precious resources, and is as far out on a limb with this project as I am. Surely he must be nervous, though he doesn't show it. How am I doing in that department, I wonder.

This big production meeting caught me off guard. I didn't know how to use it. I needed to be up-dated on the progress with the design elements, to get a measure of the cast and to sense the possibilities and the problems in rehearsal before I could make use of a huge production meeting. After some general talk the room cleared on a rather anti-climactic note, though I have to admit that Yury had demonstrated how ready and eager his company are.

The good news is that the material for the set (or some of it anyway) is in the shop and they intend to start building right away. We can't have a rake, but we will have the horseshoe second-level ramp which surrounds the stage. The Set Designer, Valery Fomin, greeted me with his soft laugh, shaking hands while taking half a step backwards, as was his habit. His sketches once again made me shake my head in admiration. With a movement of pure magic the columns of Theseus's court rise up out of the ground, pulling with them a mass of material that in turn creates the forest.[1]

Tuesday, April 3, 1990

Theseus: Merry and tragical? Tedious and brief?
  That is hot ice and wondrous strange snow.
  How shall we find the concord of this discord? (Act V, scene i)

First a catch-up chat with Andrey Shiriayev, the Assistant Director. Dressed in the same brown suit he'd worn in the fall and with the same fragile dignity, he confessed that the cast had met only once, to read the play. Little had been done on the music and the movement sessions with Oleg Kiselev had not been very productive.

Those naughty Russians! Twice I had phoned to check on progress and, protected by distance, they had assured me the whole company was eagerly preparing for the production. Andrey was too polite to be critical of Oleg, but with a little probing I got the impression the actors of the Pushkin had not taken kindly to being treated as if they were members of the Kiselev troupe. Was Oleg in some unofficial way too low on the totem pole of the hierarchy of Russian theatre artists to get away with playing the dictator? Or were the actors just too lazy? Somehow I'm sure the production is better off without him.

Finally the big moment arrived: The First Rehearsal. I had asked for the chairs to be placed in a circle. Sergei Agapitov (Puck) was in the middle of rehearsals with another company and no one at the Pushkin had bothered to make arrangements for him to be released for this first reading. Was this an attempt through deliberate negligence to force me to choose a Puck from inside the company? We've also lost, I discovered, three actors from the original cast list. Hermia is pregnant; Lysander decided after graduating to join another company; and Flute, on whom I had counted so much, is taking a directing course at a film school. I chalked all this up on my list of frustrations but didn't flinch.

Yury gave a formal speech of welcome and wished the project well. He made it sound as if I could walk on water—"brilliant international director" and so forth. I looked around the room trying to peer inside the

---

[1] Very little of this was ever realized for both budgetary and sightline reasons.

abstruse Soviet soul, taking in the looks of eagerness and boredom, pride and curiosity. The three actors standing in for the three we had lost tried hard to look keen. They knew they were on probation. The senior actors, like Valery (Theseus) and Elena (Hippolyta), affected disdain. Valery was even openly flirting with one of the young fairies next to him. Then Yury announced that Irina Biakova (Helena) had just won a prize in a recent Soviet film festival. The room broke into spontaneous and genuine applause. A lovely display of support. Irina blushed. This is a true Helena.

Working in a foreign language in a foreign country has a way of depriving one of one's senses. Most of the time it feels like trying to fight one's way out of a room full of cotton wool. But when I finally stood up to talk and realized that we had a cast, a play and a rehearsal hall, that we were going to start work, it was as if someone had adjusted the focus of a camera. Of course I attempted to echo Yury's formal tone: "What an honour this is for a Canadian to be working with such an extraordinary group of Russian actors in this great theatre.... How lucky we are to be attacking one of the great plays of the world stage together," etc. etc. I explained that for the next three days we would only be reading the play. They were not to "act," only to begin asking questions.

We began. It was totally flat, totally devoid of any concentration. They mumbled their way through without paying any attention to one another. Was this their reaction to my note? What a difference from a Canadian cast who, with only three or four weeks to rehearse, will hit the ground on the first day with its tires spinning. I interrupted the reading to ask one actor to pay attention. I asked politely the first time, less politely the next. What was going on here? My blood was starting to boil. When I again stopped the reading to inquire whether it is usual in Russian theatre to talk amongst themselves while one of their fellow actors is reading, there was a startled silence, as if to say, "But you asked us not to act." Were they having me on? My mind flipped back to an incident at the Schiller Theatre during my brief stint as assistant director in the early '70s. After the first day of rehearsal with a visiting Polish director, the senior actors sat in the actors' canteen over a beer and laid bets on how long it would take them to "do" this foreign director. Three days later the director packed his bags and left. Was I getting a version of this? How do I motivate them to want to do the play? I looked around the room and tried to figure out who was fired up and how to light a spark under those who didn't care. This is going to be a long, hard battle.

When the reading was finished (over three hours later), I launched into the short version of the concept of the production. Valentin Burov (Egeus), clearly one of the more dubious of the cast, asked, "Is this a comedy or a tragedy?" He posed the question in a sombre, self-conscious voice that made me think he was a self-appointed spokesperson for the skeptics. Was he implying the concept was too serious and not true to the comic nature of the play?

I replied that Shakespeare, particularly in his early plays, defies the easy categories of dramatic criticism. To Philostrate's description of the story of Pyramus and Thisby as "tragical mirth," Theseus responds, "Merry and tragical? Tedious and brief? / That is hot ice and wondrous strange snow. / How shall we find the concord of this discord?" The juxtaposition of opposites, the oxymoron "hot ice," is the key to understanding the nature of the Bard's early plays like *A Midsummer Night's Dream, Romeo and Juliet, The Merchant of Venice* and even, though to a lesser extent, *The Comedy of Errors.*[2] Shakespeare juggles our emotions in such a way that the comic and the tragic get close enough to each other to create a new "concord." Just as we experience a salty taste and a sweet taste on different areas of our tongue, so we experience comedy and tragedy with different parts of our being. Shakespeare, it seems to me, has the ability to put the two sensations on stage at the same moment, and the audience experiences the two realities at the same time. I used the analogy of the recently established Russian business practice of joint ventures to explain. The Soviet Union is, to use Mulroney's phrase, "open for business." It has allowed foreign companies (like McDonald's) to come in and do business in the USSR as joint ventures. However, unlike Mulroney, the Soviets never allow a foreign company to own more than fifty percent of any venture; the Soviets maintain control. It is the same in Shakespeare. We call *Romeo and Juliet* a tragedy and *A Midsummer Night's Dream* a comedy, but each contains elements of the other. Indeed, the two works were written within a short time of each other, and the story of Pyramus and Thisby is a comic duplication of the story of Romeo and Juliet. So *A Midsummer Night's Dream* is a joint venture comedy/tragedy with comedy holding the majority ownership. Theseus's court is a place where power is very real. When Theseus utters the word "death" (the Russian word is the evil-sounding *smert*), it must leap out at the characters with believable force. And the

---

[2] Antony Sher in his diary *Year of the King* mentions repeatedly how puzzled he was by all the laughs that his portrayal of Richard III was getting.

traditional folk world of the mechanicals must also be deeply rooted in reality. Thus it might be possible to move instantaneously at certain moments from tears of laughter to tears of pain.

After my talk Arkady played some of the music for us. He had solved the problem of the anthem. Many of the actors jokingly stood up because it sounded so much like the Soviet anthem.

The score at the end of the day: Oberon, Bottom, Helena and Puck will all be fine. Sergei Agapitov (Puck) had arrived half-way through the reading, shrugging sheepishly that it was not his fault. He said later that the other director had refused to let him go. As soon as he had sat down and added his voice, the quality of the reading had shot up. The actress Yury would have me use as Hermia is too old, too soft, not sexy enough. Titania and the other lovers are a serious worry. Have I got the horses to pull this through? Is the production too huge for the Pushkin? There is no sense fighting for technical and physical elements they don't have the capacity to deliver. There is no sense in driving myself mad. How do I sort out the obtainable from that which is beyond the pale? We have crossed the Rubicon. I guess there is no turning back.

Wednesday, April 4, 1990

Bottom: What beard were I best to play it in?
Quince: Why, what you will. (Act I, scene ii)

The second reading. Sergei didn't show up. A little bit more life than yesterday and the actors even grudgingly refrained from talking too much. Trying to penetrate the hearts and minds of twenty Russians through the filtered screen of a foreign language is exhausting work. They can't figure out whether to treat me as someone special because I'm from the west or to treat me with disrespect in order to rescue some of their pride. Their inability to focus on the work at hand is not a matter of a lack of interest in the production. Perhaps they expect me to behave differently? Or perhaps this is a natural behaviour pattern developed as an antidote to a totalitarian world?

Ksenia, the costume designer, has the most pride of all. I am fascinated by her talent. With a magnificent, immaculately coiffed pony-tail, she arrives late to every meeting. Today she led the traditional post-reading costume show-and-tell. She was intimidated by the large number of people and her voice barely rose above a whisper as she took the cast through her designs. Half the actors were gossiping about a party they attended the night before and some giggled at the sexually explicit costumes of the fairies. One actress asked if the Amazons will really be acting with one breast bared. Ksenia, who wants the fairies to flaunt their sexuality, ducked the issue and mumbled something about a body-stocking. Alexander Yermakov (Oberon) flatly stated that he will not wear a beard, and Elena made a stink about the colour of her costume. As they say in Russian, *Vsyo normalnie* ("everything is normal"). The actors are doing a great imitation of the clichéd reactions of the mechanicals in *A Midsummer Night's Dream*.

Thursday, April 5, 1990

Bottom: ... I will aggravate my voice so that I will roar you as gently as any sucking dove; I will roar you and 'twere any nightingale. (Act I, scene ii)

The third read-through. Am I mistaken or is there a touch more concentration and tension in the air? Oleg is discovering some of the humour in the part of Bottom. He is experimenting with his physical size and his deep voice, and is imitating a dusty, classical delivery as he recites the mock poetry. A few chuckles from the rest of the cast helped to reinforce his attempts. He is a cautious actor. He refuses to try the easy route. I must make sure he is allowed to explore and I don't force his own creative rhythms merely because I have a need to see quick results. Alexander Borovikov, a young member of the company, has been reading the part of Lysander. This morning, on a hunch, I switched him and Andrey Dubovsky, who was cast as Demetrius. It worked. I now feel that the male lovers are set. The new Hermia continues to try valiantly to impress me. It is sad to watch her efforts and know that she is so wrong. The new Flute is abominable, and Sergei didn't turn up again. I'm sure he is an alcoholic. Is he having difficulty finding his way to rehearsal? His absence is being used by a number of people as an argument to let him go. For today's reading I asked one of the female fairies, a bouncy, odd-looking actress, to read the part. She was acceptable, but not in the same league as my nasty, dwarfish alcoholic. I remember John Hirsch's words when discussing the merits of a

well-known Canadian actor: "I'm too old to work with drunks." Am I
asking for trouble?

Ouch! I've just been bitten again. As I lie here trying to make sense of
the day while fighting off sleep, I am being eaten alive by bedbugs. Like
the cockroaches in the kitchen and in the bathroom, they are citizens of
Moscow one has to learn to live with.

The Pushkin has arranged for me to eat in the restaurant in the Warsaw
Hotel. Tonight I asked Misha, the driver, to join me for supper. His dark
eyes have been following my every movement with the kind of attention
that gives me goose bumps. He seems to be trying to insinuate himself
into the heart of the production. Does he report on me to somebody?
During the meal I asked him about Gorbachev. "Gorbachev? So what?"
This is the usual reaction. The Russians don't worship the man as we do in
the west. To them he is the man who in his first year in office tried to
eliminate alcoholism by closing the breweries and destroying the vineyards.
It is going to take decades for them to grow back.

"It was like Prohibition in America," Misha said.

"What happens if he gets shot?" I inquired.

"So he gets shot," he quipped.

"Is anyone going to shoot him?"

"Well, maybe yes, maybe no."

"And what would happen if he were shot?"

"Oh, who cares!"

This casual cynicism and assumption that the future of the Soviet
Union is not for the average person to determine are the norm. I made
one last attempt to engage him in a serious discussion: "What about
Lithuania?"

With some vehemence he snapped back, "Well, they can't just go their
own way. What about all these people who don't want to separate? Lithuania can't just walk out of the Union."

Misha, it turns out, is a deputy in one of the local Moscow Soviets.
How did this oleaginous individual become a public deputy? It does not
seem to take up much of his time.[3]

---

[3] We were pulled over a couple of times during the month by the traffic police (the
Gaï) for speeding. Misha flashed his ID which was enough to free him on the spot from
further questioning.

Friday, April 6, 1990

*Quince: Come, sit down, every mother's son, and rehearse your parts.
(Act III, scene i)*

The morning ride to the theatre is fifty minutes long. The final turn off
Gorky Street takes us by the new McDonald's. Even before opening time,
the street is jammed with patient Muscovites standing in line for a bite of a
western hamburger. Forty minutes is said to be the average wait. Overlooking Pushkin Square opposite the Big Mac Factory is Moscow's first capitalist neon sign, a big red Coca-Cola proudly flashing like the flag of a
conquering army over the captured citadel of the enemy. Soviet revenge:
I've yet to see the sign without at least a couple of circuits out of order.

    The first half of the morning was spent talking through the mechani-
cals' scenes. We located a few places where Bottom's malapropisms are not
translated with the full value of their double entendres, but we found no
solutions. We also couldn't find a name for the character of Bottom which
includes the anatomical pun. Then we talked about the individual characters, and I asked Yuri Rumiantcev what he thought about the idea of
playing Quince as an idealistic, Jewish, intellectual carpenter, a pedant and
slow-moving craftsman with a predilection for detail and accuracy, who
measures everything twice before he cuts. Yuri had seen Ksenia's costume
sketch which made the character look exactly like Trotsky. I could see that
as an actor he is both intrigued and challenged but he is also a little
apprehensive about the ramifications of playing a Jew in the Russia of
today. He gave a cautious assent to the idea. For the character of Bottom I
asked if there was a particular accent that represented the heart of rural
Russia, an accent that would immediately be recognized as that of a typical
Russian worker. They unanimously agreed that the somewhat comic but
distinct Volga accent, with its different "o" and "a" sounds, would do the
trick. Oleg grinned at the idea. They suggested he could be a *grushnik*, a
Jack-of-all-trades but master of none. This kind of man hangs around the
beer hall, hoists the occasional bit of cargo on trucks or in warehouses and
generally talks more than he works. The actor playing Snug asked if he
could play the role as a Ukrainian. This suggestion sent everyone into a
paroxysm of laughter. Is a Ukrainian a kind of Soviet Newfie?

    We played around a little with the mechanicals' first scene. They have a
terrible habit of improvising and adding to the text. I explained that the

fact that their dialogue is written in prose does not give them the licence to muddle it up. They nodded in acknowledgement and continued in their previous sloppy mode. In the Folio edition of the play the stage direction at the top of Act Three, scene one, actually reads: "Enter the clownes." In other words these characters must be understood as clowns and I would like to layer in one or two routines—pie in the face, pratfalls and so on. To this end I have asked the theatre to provide us with the services of a clown teacher from the Moscow Circus. The actors, I discovered, have been totally negligent about learning how to play their instruments. Arkady's wonderful music is all for naught at the moment.

The second half of the day was spent with Oberon, Titania and (believe it or not) Puck. Alexander Yermakov, tall and with a steely sexual presence, will make a great Oberon. He asks all the right questions and it is clear he has honed his personal methodology for approaching parts. Some of the actors understand at least a little English and follow what I am saying before it is translated. Alexander doesn't understand a word. But he keeps his eyes on me as I talk as if this will help him soak up my true intent. His eyes flick nervously every now and then over to whomever is interpreting as if to say, "Am I understanding this correctly?" He is not a singer but loves the idea of the text being supported by the music. The bigger the back-up and the harder the rock, the better, as far as he is concerned. Maria Zubareva, as Titania, is the opposite. Timid in her approach to the role, she mumbles the text and doesn't experiment with anything. With her small voice, she is afraid of the music, and the long "These are the forgeries of jealousy" speech petrifies her. Every idea I throw at her seems to scare her backwards rather than forwards. Sergei is still fighting the director of the other theatre to get time off to be with us. We sorted out a time-sharing proposal that he will take to the other company.

Arkady keeps shaking his head over Sergei's voice: "I've never heard a man sing that high!" The music tape he put together for these three characters is terrible. With a cheap Russian synthesizer and unimaginative rhythms he went into a studio and ended up with music that sounds worse than any advertising jingle. I had suggested music that would give the monologues some magical underpinning and support what the actors are doing. He has created elevator music. On the drive to the theatre this morning I had taken Misha's favourite Rolling Stones tape out of the car's tape deck and popped in Arkady's music. Misha had listened for a short while and then snorted with glee: "Do you like that? It is boring!" Would the melodic lines be acceptable if we let the actors sing a cappella? Perhaps the spells should have live accompaniment rather than taped music?

Again it hit me what a big production this is by Pushkin standards. I'm desperate for more rehearsal time. We can work only from eleven to three every day and then in the evening I get only those actors who are not performing. Sasha[4] (Oberon) has a genuine commitment to the project, and this gives me back the energy to plow on. After rehearsal Orlov assured me the Pushkin will do anything to accommodate the sponsor: signs in the lobby, company name on the marquee, logo in the program.

The day ended at Ksenia's finalizing the military uniforms and the "clown" costumes. The front door of her apartment is blackened and charred (it had been that way the first time I visited) and I finally felt comfortable enough to ask her what had happened. She lives with her parents and her thirteen-year-old daughter. Her father is Jewish. It is possible, she said, that they were the victims of an anti-Semitic organization called *Pamyat* ("Memory"). This right wing, nationalist organization holds the Jews responsible for the evils of the Revolution and they are determined to make them pay. To join one has to volunteer the names and addresses of five Jews. Ksenia's daughter had been home alone when the fire was started but luckily a neighbour discovered it and put it out before the fire had time to spread. In the same apartment block, apparently, another Jewish family had been burned to death in a similar incident. Ksenia related the whole story with a baffling casualness. It took me a few moments to realize what she had been saying. There is so much hatred and bottled tension in this country. Where will it end? Ksenia shrugged her shoulders.

Saturday, April 7, 1990

Theseus: Lovers and madmen have such seething brains,
   Such shaping fantasies, that apprehend
   More than cool reason ever comprehends. (Act V, scene i)

I'm sitting in one of my favourite places in the Pushkin, the director's box overlooking the stage and adjacent to Yury's office. There is something enlivening for an artistic director about having such direct access to the

---

[4] As we became friends, Alexander Yermakov became "Sasha." Russians love diminutives.

work. Elena Shumskaya, the Stage Manager, is on the deck screaming at the stage-hands because the children's matinée starts in twenty minutes and the set isn't up yet. The stage-hands calmly maintain their snail's pace. Elena does not have the authority a stage manager has in the English theatre system. Our stage managers are the centre of communication, planning and organization in rehearsal. Here there is no comparable central position. These functions seem to be divided with no apparent logic between the assistant director, the assistant to the artistic director and the stage manager. Can I cope with this chaos?

I'm having a cup of tea and eating a biscuit—I mean a cookie (my days in England leave their legacy). This cookie is fairly good. It is made by the State bakery and comes wrapped in a fairly plain package. Now, if this were the west, the same cookie would be packaged with considerably more marketing flair. Would I then think the cookie tasted better? I'm reminded as I sit munching the cookie that the Soviet system was built on a very idealistic belief in human intelligence, on the belief that a good product will sell itself. In the west no one ever goes broke overestimating the gullibility of the consumer; Russia is going broke because of too much faith in reason. Lenin and Trotsky built their nation on the mistaken assumption that human nature could be purely rational. Unfortunately, we are competitive, we are irrationally driven, we have dark, unexplored nooks and crannies in our internal "forest." To quote Theseus, we "apprehend more than cool reason comprehends." Doing *A Midsummer Night's Dream* here and now is important. But will a Russian audience ever perceive that?

Shakespeare is writing from the perspective of a world run by men. The play begins with Theseus's defeat of the female kingdom of the Amazons. Then Oberon through his superior power charms Titania into falling in love with an ass and thereby wins the argument over the changeling boy. How does one in the '90s search for wisdom in these relationships? Is Oberon in fact weak because he *has* to win? Does he lose by winning? Sasha seems to have the courage to explore some of these questions but Masha[5] is still a stranger to me.

In the evening I ended up in the basement studio of a young theatre designer who had worked with Canadian-American director Des McAnuff on a production of Des's play *The Death of Von Richthoven as Witnessed from Earth*. It had been scheduled for the Sovremennik Theatre and Des had been over four times to work on the show only to have it suddenly

---

[5] "Masha" is a diminutive form of "Maria."

cancelled. Oooopps! That sent a tremor of anxiety through the veins. Des had brought over his production of *A Walk in the Woods* (in English), the Broadway play about the Geneva disarmament talks. The reception had apparently split down east/west lines with all the Americans in Moscow loving the show while the Soviets were appalled at the simplicity of the writing.

Sunday, April 8, 1990

Puck: What hempen home-spuns have we swagg'ring here, (Act III, scene i)

On weekends most of the company is involved in the two children's matinées, which means I have few actors to rehearse with. So today I went to Gorky Park. It is more a tired facsimile of a small-town agricultural fair than a big-city amusement park. The rides are ancient and foreign-built. I ventured into something called the "180° Vision." We stood in the middle of a tent watching a 180° screen on which various hair-raising journeys were projected. The camera had been placed on the front of roller-coasters, racing cars and low-flying airplanes. Watching this, my body was tricked into reactions, resembling those of a drunk on a fishing boat in a hurricane. Yet all around me the Russians stood stock still, as if the cinematic effects weren't even registering. Is their sense perception not hooked up to their motor mechanism as tightly as ours is because of the political system under which they live?

Later we managed to find a little time for the mechanicals to meet the circus instructor for the first time. He is a very old-fashioned Russian in faded clothes and with an obsession with status. He kept genuflecting with his cap in hand like some old Irish peasant. I put him on the stage and he began to talk.

"The basis of clowning is truth. If you try to be funny you will fail. If you go for truth you will become a clown." The usual tried and true stuff.

The actors nodded. (Not all were there, of course. The original Snout, a wonderfully crotchety old actor, had been replaced without explanation by a younger, totally talentless man. The substitute Flute, Vladimir Grigorev, was disgustingly ingratiating and drove me crazy.) The clown teacher went on. "I have watched many younger students try to become clowns and the ones who succeeded were the ones who had found the clown in themselves."

This helped support everything I was telling them about looking for the real human being in their characters. More talk but no work. Except that talk is how we work.

Monday, April 9, 1990

Demetrius: But like a sickness did I loathe this food;
    But, as in health, come to my natural taste,
    Now I do wish it, love it, long for it. (Act IV, scene i)

Our day off. As we rounded the corner and passed McDonald's this morning I saw there was no line-up. This seemed like the right time to play the tourist on a fact-finding mission and have a Big Mac. Like some grotesque parody Moscow's McDonald's out-McDonald's any North American franchise I've ever seen. There must be a hundred freshly scrubbed Russian youths behind the counter, all outfitted in neat purple uniforms and shouting madly at the customers as they enter, "Over here! Over here!"

You call out your order as you brush by the Canadian flag at the entrance and by the time you reach the counter it is ready. A Big Mac, fries, tea and an apple turnover cost the equivalent of two days' wages for an actor. It tasted exactly as it tastes in T.O. (That is an awesome feat!) And five minutes after I'd eaten I got exactly the same indigestion as I would have in Toronto.

Did Puck squeeze some magic drops in my eyes last night? Here I have been complaining about the ugliness and dirtiness of Moscow. Today I saw it as beautiful. As Valera,[6] the Set Designer, drove us along the banks of the Moskva River the sun came out and gave the buildings an elegance I hadn't seen before. We stopped at a hillside monastery outside town. Moscow's Nôtre Dame, Valera explained. In the distance the skyline of Moscow, across the river rows and rows of vegetable fields being cultivated. An extraordinarily peaceful and human scene. Looking out over the river winding at our feet and the barges gliding past, Valera began to bemoan the future of Russia.

"Nothing has changed in five years. Nothing is going to change without violence." Last week, he said, two police detectives, deputies in the

---

[6] "Valera" is a diminutive form of "Valery."

Leningrad Soviet, who had been investigating corruption in the upper echelons of the Party, had been due to appear on television to make certain allegations. They had apparently traced corruption right up as high as Ligachov in the Politburo. At the scheduled time the announcer introduced the two detectives and then the screen went blank. Five minutes later a documentary on skiing was aired. The next day the Leningrad Soviet fired the director of the television station for pulling the plug on the program and had it rescheduled for later that day. At the appointed time the screen once again went blank. Then the detectives themselves were charged and the Soviet is debating whether or not deputies are immune before the law. For the first time these deliberations are being debated on television. During the week following Valera's disclosure of all this, nobody at the theatre would talk of anything else.[7] In my apartment at night I caught some of the sessions, which looked like a badly run high school debating society. If this was the rudimentary beginnings of some kind of democracy, then things had better speed up if they want to head chaos off at the pass. It looks to me like a race against time that is sure to be lost. Is it any wonder that theatre in Moscow has so little focus when the real drama is being played out in everyday life?

Tuesday, April 10, 1990

Philostrate: ... in all the play
    There is not one word apt, one player fitted. (Act V, scene i)

Thank God *A Midsummer Night's Dream* is a play that can hide the deficiencies of a company of actors. If I can carefully encourage each actor to find an area of his or her capabilities that is truthful, yet strongly enough defined to live inside the visually powerful concept of the production, then the action of the play will mask the inadequacies of the cast.

Oleg Antonov invited me to see him play Lopakhin in a production of *The Cherry Orchard*. It is a co-operative sponsored by a Swiss cultural institute and the actors are "stars" from a range of the major theatres in Moscow who perform on their free evenings. Because this private venture

---

[7] One day as I was passing by I peeked into the smoke-filled crew room to find what appeared to be the entire staff of the Pushkin crowded in front of the only available television.

is doing so well and the tickets are more expensive than for the State-financed theatres, the actors can be paid exorbitant sums by Moscow standards (the equivalent of two weeks' wages for one performance). Having seen the Schaubuehne production of *The Cherry Orchard* directed by Peter Stein, I went with some apprehension. (There will surely never be a better production in this century.)

The evening turned out worse than I feared: all Lyubimov's tricks thrown together incoherently by a young director—abrupt changes of pace, rhythm and focus that make it impossible to follow the text, and actors screaming at the audience and performing business which destroys the credibility of the characters. This play depends to a great extent upon a careful observation of the Russian class system before the Revolution. Are Russians not interested in their own history? The abandon with which they destroy this classic and the excessive worship of gratuitous spontaneity must be a reaction to the strait-jacket of contemporary Russian life. There is no real interest in the text. The actor playing Firs, a revered, older Moscow actor, floated through the mayhem like a ghost of theatre past. He caught that unique Chekhovian (and very Shakespearean) compound of comedy and tragedy in which the character's own ambitions expose both a comic self-ridicule and a tragic inevitability. Oleg played Lopakhin with a charming obsequiousness that seemed irrelevant to anything else that was going on. Tomorrow I'll have to find some bland niceness to say to him and hope he'll forgive me for not liking the show.

Wednesday, April 11, 1990

Bottom: The eye of man hath not heard, the ear of man hath not seen, man's hand is not able to taste, his tongue to conceive, nor his heart to report, what my dream was. (Act IV, scene i)

With the mechanicals I tried to pursue our understanding of the nature of comedy and tragedy. Is sight the dominant sense in comedy? Is comedy a process of understanding through observation whereas tragedy is a process of physical "knowing" through feeling? In *Dream* at moments of tension or great emotion Shakespeare has his characters' senses constantly cross-perceive phenomena. Bottom's "I see a voice" (Act Five, scene one) usually gets a big laugh from the house. Has Shakespeare in entwining comedy and tragedy also confused the sense perception of the audience? It is extraordinary that a play generally accepted as a lighter comedy has as its central image an ass making love to a woman. In rural communities the ass, though sterile, is celebrated for the size of its penis. Now, let your mind roam towards some darker fantasies and you will marvel that Shakespeare has been able to camouflage this play as family entertainment.

More talk in the evening. At the top of Act Five, Theseus and Hippolyta are discussing the fantastic stories the four lovers have been telling about the events in the forest. Theseus categorically dismisses them as untrue: "I never may believe / These antique fables, nor these fairy toys." I explained to Valery Barinov that the Duke refuses to understand or even acknowledge the chaos of the forest and the night because it is a world he cannot rule over.

"Ah, yes," Valery replied, "Theseus is a Marxist-Leninist. He thinks like a Marxist-Leninist."

Bull's-eye! He has caught the essence of the production. Hippolyta replies to Theseus, "But all the story of the night told over ... grows to something of great constancy." As a woman she has the ability to perceive other dimensions in the world. Elena Skorokhodova is beginning to see the male/female division in the play and is enjoying doing battle with both Theseus the character and Valery the actor.

Marianna, Yury's assistant, is a single parent earning seven roubles a day. She has ration cards for sugar, but there is no sugar available in the government stores. In fact, as the Soviet Union moves toward a projected June transition to a market economy,[8] there is less and less food of any kind obtainable in the government stores. At Moscow's tiny private enterprise markets oranges are fifteen to twenty roubles a kilo. All this the consequence of rationality taken to an extreme.

Thursday, April 12, 1990

Theseus: For never any thing can be amiss,
   When simpleness and duty tender it. (Act V, scene i)

After the morning rehearsal a visit to the Novodevichii Monastery where, adjacent to its walls and shaded by the boughs of ancient, gnarled trees, lie

---

[8] As of February 1, 1991, this transition still hadn't happened.

buried the "Who's Who" of Moscow's past. One section is devoted to the communist military heroes whose graves are marked by large replicas of tanks and warships. Across a narrow path, more tightly packed and more moss-covered, are the graves of the cultural world. Together again are the founders of the Moscow Art Theatre, Stanislavsky and Nemirovich-Danchenko. Not far away are Chekhov and his wife, Olga Knipper. I had come to tender my respects to Tairov and his wife, Aliisa Koonin. After Stalin had hijacked his theatre, Tairov (so Moscow theatre lore has it) went mad and would walk up and down the street in front of the Pushkin, accosting passers-by with the declaration, "I used to run that theatre, you know." He died a year later. Out of revenge his wife put a curse on the theatre. Since that time, I've been told, the Pushkin has produced little of artistic merit.

According to the same lore, if you are directing at the Pushkin you must ask Tairov's wife to remove the curse temporarily. I placed some roses on the grave and buried a copy of DeWitt's drawing of the Swan Theatre in the dirt over her grave. I believe absolutely that the spirits of the founders and the major influences of a theatre hover over the stage. It is very important that both Aliisa and Tairov understand and be sympathetic to what we are trying to do. But my mind was troubled, I felt awkward, and I don't think I was able to reach her. I determined that on my next visit to Moscow I would return and again try to talk to her. I wonder if Yury's attempts to celebrate the beginnings of the Kammerni by repainting the lobby and so on are part of a ploy to deflect the curse.

This evening I worked with the lovers and Puck on some of the forest scenes. We have worked out an acceptable routine with Sergei's other rehearsals, and he is now with us regularly. Standing all of four feet, in a well-worn red tracksuit and his hair dishevelled, Sergei can be a touch obstreperous, especially if he has had a drink before rehearsals. Yes, he will be a handful. I suggested to Alexei (Alexander) that Demetrius might have been born with a birthmark on his face. He really disliked the idea. I suspect that being a bit of a hunk in real life he doesn't want to be ugly on stage. I tried to explain it might be a gift to him as an actor to have such a mark of imperfection. Surely this might make sense of the character's psychology, his constant need to strut and beat his chest, his constant challenging of Lysander to fight, and his need to win Hermia, whom I see as the spoiled rich kid of their world. Alexei remained skeptical. We did manage to explore some of the physical relationships in the forest, however; the young actors throw themselves about with an alarming abandon and I think there is blocking we can hang on to for the future. Helena has some nice moments when she kicks the two guys in the groin. Alexei is developing Demetrius as a kung fu expert. A Russian send-up of Bruce Lee could be very funny. Now if only we had a Hermia.

Friday, April 13, 1990

Hermia: ... look how I do quake with fear.
  Methought a serpent eat my heart away, (Act II, scene ii)

As far as rehearsals go, a total write-off. Half the company is on tour somewhere in the provinces. This is how the actors supplement their meagre income. The business of Hermia came to a head. I had auditioned the girls from the first year of the Moscow Art Theatre School (the class Yury intends to take into the Pushkin when they graduate and the same students who will be playing the fairies and the soldiers in my production). One of the students seemed worth a try, so I asked her to rehearsal today for the first time. When Vera Leskova, who has been working on the part for the last ten days, walked in and saw me talking to the student, she knew exactly what was happening and fled to her dressing-room in hysterics. Andrey, the Assistant Director, just shrugged his shoulders: "That's her problem." I followed her to explain, but she couldn't look at me and covered her face in shame. She's a decent actress, just wrong for the part.

The change-over was handled with no consideration for her feelings and I felt very guilty. The stage manager and the assistant director had assured me there would be no problem. "This is her job, she will understand, she doesn't need any special treatment." They even opposed my going to her dressing-room to see her. It didn't seem as if anything I said helped her deal with the situation.

Suddenly during this crisis I crashed full force against the language barrier. Up to now I had enjoyed the mystique of giving an actor a note and then watching carefully as he/she received it in translation. I could usually see from the reaction in the eyes whether the actor understood, and what he/she thought of it. The extra step in communication actually gave me more time to watch the workings of the actors as they responded to the ideas. And if they misunderstood and took the note in the wrong way it was easy to see this from the acting and then to simply give the note in another manner. My comprehension of Russian has improved since I arrived but I don't let the actors know how much I really understand in order to gain a few extra moments to deal with any situation. When I have thrown out the odd word or phrase in Russian they've laughed in surprise. Today, however, I would have given anything not to have had to use an interpreter.

Andrey maintains there are no talented young female actors in Moscow. They can either buy or sleep their way into theatre school so few with talent or integrity get in. At any rate, despite the crisis and with the new Hermia, we did some good work with the lovers. Andrey Dubovsky has developed some nice character detail for Lysander in the first scene with Hermia. He wipes his glasses as he says in a pedantic, bookish tone, "For aught that I could ever read, / Could ever hear by tale of history, / The course of true love never did run smooth." And Demetrius is enjoying strutting through the forest like some high school jock-hero. Rough justice is then meted out to the two young men when the spells are placed on them and they are forced to crawl on their knees begging Helena for her love.

Sasha continues to play Oberon as though he were a character in a Chekhov play. He destroys the rhythms of the lines and whispers or mumbles the text. I once again attempted to impress upon him that the czar of the underworld has an image to maintain. At least Sasha has true concentration. He has actually bothered to put his script in book form for easier handling in rehearsal. The Pushkin doesn't have the resources to provide all the actors with a full script so most of them walk around with bits and pieces of typed pages that end up lost or in the wrong order. Half the time Alexander Borovikov is on the wrong page or giving the wrong cue. Is this sloppiness, indifference or just normal Russian behaviour?

After rehearsal Ksenia and I went through the costume storage racks to look for suitable costumes for the Pyramus and Thisby interlude. A surprisingly small assortment for such a large theatre with such a long production history. The uniforms they want to pull for the soldiers look very unreal. I insisted on the need for veracity. Ksenia has seen the material the theatre has purchased to make the fairy costumes. It is not the real leather she asked for and she is livid. Is this where I am supposed to thump the table and demand things? Seeing everywhere evidence of how financially hard up the theatre is I feel it would be wrong to ask them to spend their scarce resources.

Assia has arrived! Back in Russia for another visit, having timed her arrival to coincide with the rehearsals, she puffed her way up four flights of stairs to the rehearsal hall. Her schizophrenia about Russia is already rampant, even though she has been back only a couple of days. She loves the people, their warmth and openness and the constant talk and hunger to communicate, but like a normal westerner she curses the slowness of the doormen and the waiters. The routine at the Hotel Warsaw is almost comic. Every day we arrive to eat, every day the same doorman tries to stop us from entering. We explain that we have special permission from the manager to eat there, the doorman says, "I don't know you," and then we send for the manager to explain to the doorman that we are allowed inside. Assia gets furious at the deliberate stupidity and rudeness. It is such a great relief to finally sit down at the table knowing that one is likely to get something to eat. Then the fights start with the waiters to get service.

In the evening Sergei finally brought in his skateboard. I'd asked him several times to show me how he was getting on with it and he hadn't complied. I was beginning to think he might have sold it for cash. The board would be worth a pretty rouble on the street. His size and his circus background make him ideally suited to be a good skateboard artist, but it was clear he had done little practising. Of course I pushed him to keep at it because even from the little we could do in the rehearsal hall it was obvious to me that this Puck on a skateboard will really work. We also experimented with Sergei singing some of the spells a cappella, but keeping the melodic line Arkady had written. Clearing out the predictable elevator music and focussing on the internal emotion of the actor singing was a little like exposing a sculpture by opening up the packing case. Arkady looked puzzled but agreed it was better. Sergei nervously looked from Arkady to me, then quietly mumbled that he liked the new way. Puck could steal the show.

Sunday, April 15, 1990

Quince: Bless thee, Bottom, bless thee! Thou art translated. (Act III, scene i)

As most of the company is still on tour, yesterday and today were wasted. The new Hermia is too inexperienced to work out, so I am again looking for the right one. Arrghh! Yury invited me to watch him audition the graduating class of GITIS, the State-run theatre school. The students demonstrated a marvellous mixture of imagination, sophomoric humour, desire to please, smart-ass cockiness and inexperience. They are going to leave their school full of an innocent confidence that they have the talent to show the established theatre world what real theatre is. Fortunately three of the girls are worth auditioning for the part of Hermia.

Met Tatyana Borisova and Sergei Tsvetkov, the new movement coaches-cum-choreographers. A husband and wife team: she with a very Gallic passion and the lithe look of a Parisian fashion model, he more introverted, with the body of a flyweight Olympic wrestler. We talked about the concept and I gave them a tape with some of the music to take away and ingest.

The evening was very special. Valera has taken us under his wing. He wants to ensure that we see some traditional Russian culture to help us understand what the country might have been, what it might yet be. So he took us all to an Easter service in a small church near the Taganka Theatre. In the Russian Orthodox tradition Christ rises on Saturday at midnight. For a couple of hours beforehand the choir sings and priests read scriptures. At the "iron tongue of midnight" the bells start ringing. The priests, carrying icons, the altar boys and the choir move in a procession through the congregation, outside the church and all around it.

As they return indoors each member of the congregation lights a candle and suddenly there is a marvellous festival of light. *Khristos Voskres.* Christ has risen. The effect is stunning. It is easily one of the most theatrical religious rituals in the world. Well before midnight the Taganka church became so tightly packed with rotund Russian matrons, whose experience and talents with hip-checks and elbowing were far beyond anything I had learned to cope with in old-timer hockey, that my claustrophobia got the better of me. (In Russian churches there are no pews—you stand.) Outside the hundreds of Muscovites unable to get into the church were being controlled by worried militiamen who were having a difficult time maintaining order and a pleasant mien.

Up in the bell tower a priest rang the bells which accompanied the procession. He seemed to have a limp or a physical defect of some kind. With extraordinary speed and stamina he ran between the five bells clanging out a continuous rhythm, while below the clergy, proudly displaying the precious icons, circumnavigated the church along a path cleared by the militia. "Cling cling" went the small bells. "Dong" went the big one, as the medieval-looking, black-robed figure frantically flitted about in the tower. The procession re-entered the church and the crowd surged forward to catch a glimpse of the candles being lit inside. The spectacle of the light spilling forth from the windows and onto the eager faces was like an illustration in a Dickens novel. *Khristos Voskres.* What kind of Christ do they think has arisen? A merciful one? A generous one? A wrathful one? Each Muscovite, I am sure, had a personal agenda for Christ that night. A friend of Assia's daughter who had remained inside the crowded church had some of her hair accidentally set on fire by a candle. It is a wonder that churches don't burn to the ground at Easter.

Afterwards we had the customary post-service feast at the home of one of Valera's friends. A large colour TV silently carried the transmission of a service in one of the cathedrals while we chewed over the future of Russia yet again. The well-worn jokes made the rounds: A Russian and an American are having an argument about whose country is better.

The American boasts loudly, "I can walk into the White House any day of the week and say that George Bush is an asshole."

"This is nothing," replies the Russian. "I can walk into the Kremlin any day of the week and also say that Bush is an asshole."

Tamara's friend (the one whose hair caught fire) is from the Ukraine. A cousin of hers lived close to Chernobyl and at the time of the nuclear disaster he and his neighbours were awakened in the middle of the night to dig up earth, transport it and dump it on the site. They had no idea why they were doing this and they had no choice but to obey. With his flesh deteriorating and his vital systems ceasing to function, the cousin is now close to death. The doctors have shown little interest in helping him in any way, the woman told us.

Monday, April 16, 1990

Titania: If you will patiently dance in our round,
  And see our moonlight revels, go with us; (Act II, scene i)

The day started with a frustrating session with Tanya (short for Tatyana) and Sergei, the choreographers. They didn't seem to have listened to the tape, nor had any of the discussion from the other day made an impression. We were working with Yury's first-year students, trying to find a sense of the physical life of the forest, what the fairies' internal rhythms were and how they translated into walking and dancing. Tanya and Sergei have achieved an extraordinary symbiosis, she with her pushy energy, he with a more introverted observer's persona. But they kept suggesting movement that was athletic, gymnastic. They don't understand these are urban fairies, not rural ones. We agonized over some Russian equivalent for the word "cool." There is none.

This evening Assia's daughter Tamara threw a party at her apartment. Risking resentment we deliberately invited only those actors with whom I am enjoying working. For many of them the western-outfitted apartment in the diplomatic compound was the closest they had ever been to heaven. At one point in the evening Elena (Hippolyta) needed to go to the bathroom. The sight of this bathroom, basic by western standards, with its simple white tiles and enamel bathtub and sink, caused her to take a step backwards and whisper to herself, "Oh, my God! It's so beautiful." Oleg and Sasha, downing the limitless quantities of western beer, made countless toasts to theatre, to work and to women. It was painful to watch the wounded look in their eyes as they tried to come to grips with why one half of the world should have all these luxuries and not them. They very kindly stayed on until midnight to sing me "Happy Birthday."

Tuesday, April 17, 1990

Theseus: Hippolyta, I woo'd thee with my sword,
  And won thy love doing thee injuries;
  But I will wed thee in another key,
  With pomp, with triumph, and with revelling. (Act I, scene i)

The first day on the stage with some of the set elements laid out. The metal ramps that surround the central playing area were fitted with some rather jerry-rigged platforms on top. Because the sides were hidden in behind the proscenium, I suggested to Valera they be angled in a touch so we could see the actors better. I tried to block the beginning of the play: Theseus's soldiers leading out the captive Amazons, Theseus proposing to Hippolyta and freeing her women when she agrees to the marriage. (In the text this has actually happened off-stage, before the play starts, but because it is very important the audience understand there has been a battle, I have chosen to illustrate it with a silent prelude.) I wanted a rough sketch of the movement to be laid out so that Tanya and Sergei could go off and develop it further. One of the soldiers refused to point his rifle at the Amazons. "I don't point rifles at human beings," he said.

Hardly an attitude that can be faulted in real life, but on the stage the consequence would be the exclusion of about half the world's dramatic literature. It was a deliberately provocative statement from a walk-on trying to demonstrate his progressive views.[9] I didn't have the time for a lengthy argument so I let it pass. Then another of the walk-ons, who is annoyed because in other plays she actually has some lines but in this production has none, was also deliberately disruptive. This isn't new. From the start of rehearsals she has never been around when she is needed, she performs all her actions with annoying slowness, and she tries to engage the other actors in conversation, particularly Valery, when they are supposed to be rehearsing. I can sense the cast watching to see how I react to this behaviour. I will bide my time and throw her out at a suitable moment. By the end of the frustrating morning session we had something roughed out and the choreographers went off to ponder how to refine it.

The evening rehearsals, on the other hand, during which we focus on the text and the motivation of the principal actors, are a delight at the

---

[9] This attitude ended up being translated in the production during the curtain call when the soldiers pile their weapons on the stage and shake hands.

moment. It is a real pleasure to be exploring without the menace of deadlines hanging over the work. These are creative rhythms to which my artistic sensibility would like to become accustomed in the future.

Wednesday, April 18, 1990

Titania: Methought I was enamour'd of an ass. (Act IV, scene i)

It is now past the middle of the month. We have achieved a lot less than I had hoped and I am totally confused. A couple of times today I wondered if I should throw in the towel. Then something would happen to spark my interest. Partly it is just that I am fucking homesick, and partly it is the wearisome, mind-numbing disorganization of this country that turns the slightest difficulty into an ordeal. Rehearsals are scheduled to start at eleven a.m., but the actors only arrive on stage at ten minutes past and then stand around with blank looks, wondering what they are supposed to be rehearsing because nothing is posted anywhere. I'm never sure who will actually turn up, as the assistant director has the only official call sheet, and often actors are excused for some reason or other. Do they think I am a wimp because I have not thrown a tyrannical fit? Should I insist that Yury come in and read the riot act? The organization should be the concern of the stage manager but, as I've established, Elena doesn't have the power.

The evening session, first with only Sasha and then with Oleg, gave me back the energy to keep going, thanks to their craft and imagination. With Sasha I talked about the self-marketing image Oberon must maintain, both to his subjects on the stage and to the audience. To help wean Sasha from his naturalistic cadences, I asked him to speak all Oberon's lines as though they were being recorded for posterity. I insisted he not take breaks in the middle of the lines, but keep the rhythms of delivery as they are laid out on the page. The Shakespearean line division is most often also a thought division, and the Russian translation has kept the integrity of this congruence. I explained that if he models his delivery along the structure of the lines, then the thoughts become clearer. We looked closely at Oberon's speech just before he wakes Titania up and decided to try to approach it as a journey towards Oberon's total surrender to her. Does he realize, looking down at her asleep in Bottom's arms, that although he has won the changeling boy by using his superior magic, he will not win her unless he surrenders himself to her? Has his trick rebounded upon himself? Is he threatened by the possibility that Titania has experienced an erotic satisfaction with Bottom? That perhaps the ass's prick was bigger and he gave her a better ride? If true love is a temporary suspension of any power relationship between two people, must Oberon go on his knees in front of her when he says, "Now Titania, wake up my sweet Queen," and give himself to her? Sasha likes having problems like this to masticate. After rehearsal he went off purring like a BMW.

With Oleg I worked on Bottom's waking-up scene in Act Four after the fairies have left. Snoring in the middle of an erotic dream, he reaches for Titania and in doing so rolls off the ramp and is jolted awake by his fall. Because of the presence of the audience, who act as the mirror he plays to in order to bolster his macho self-image, this is a moment of complete humiliation. His speech, then, is his attempt to regain his self-confidence: "I have had a dream, past the wit of man to say what dream it was" becomes the base camp from which he begins the assault on the heights of his former self-glorification. Oleg hits and misses as he looks for the size of the character. Once he finds the size he refuses on principle to repeat it—an actor's methodology that values the creative process and refuses to succumb to routine. I've asked him to go to a farm or a zoo to study the actions of an ass so that certain ass-like movement patterns enter into the portrayal of the part. At the end of the session a few of the other mechanicals arrived to work on the reunion of Bottom with his friends in Act Four. Bottom is caught between wanting to boast of his conquest of Titania and being uncertain about whether the story will make him look like an ass. Nina (Starveling) at 5' and Oleg at 6'3" are beginning to develop an onstage friendship which could turn into a nice comic team. Both the composer and the musical director sat on the stage next to me during some of the rehearsal and laughed themselves silly.

Thursday, April 19, 1990

Bottom: Where are these lads? Where are these hearts? (Act IV, scene ii)

Twice today I threw in the towel. First when the actor playing Wall didn't turn up again for the morning's rehearsal. He is taking over a major role in a Dostoevsky piece and management has decreed without consulting me that he could skip our work. When we nevertheless tried to start the play-within-the-play, none of the other actors had his/her script or knew whose lines were next. And the substitute Wall is a breath-takingly terrible actor. The second towel got thrown in during the evening rehearsals. Maria (Titania) didn't show up because her second husband refused to baby-sit her child from her first marriage. The music for the Titania/Oberon *pas de deux* in Act Four was not ready and the choreographers are still coming up with movement that is suitable for a gymnastics event, but not our production. I went to the Direktor's office and spat out, "This is a waste of my valuable time."

Orlov nodded in his best father confessor manner and replied, "What can I do to help?"

"At least get the fucking actors to rehearsal," I barked. (It's great to swear and leave the poor interpreter with the problem of softening the language.)

"I'll talk to Yury about this," Orlov assured me.

I pulled Sasha aside later and asked him on the q.t. what I should be doing.

"Yury has to sort this out. It is his problem. The lack of organization, the lack of responsibility, are his problems."

Why aren't these Russian actors inspired by their first opportunity to tackle a Shakespeare? Aren't they hungry and excited to try something different? No chance. They turn the poetry to prose. This is, I believe, a deliberate reaction to the old-fashioned, dusty, nineteenth-century Russian theatre which turned everything into heightened language and boring declamation. Now they are afraid to give the poetry its true size. On days like today I feel like a foreigner getting the deliberately disdainful treatment of a spiteful waiter in a State restaurant. I refuse to get angry, though. I didn't come here to become a kindergarten teacher to a bunch of unruly kids.

Friday, April 20, 1990

Hermia: Methinks I see these things with parted eye,
*   When every thing seems double. (Act IV, scene i)*

Maria showed up with all her lines down, apologizing for missing last night. Arkady brought in some very sexy music for the *pas de deux*, the real actor playing Wall was in rehearsal, and Tanya and Sergei had Puck jump on Bottom's shoulders during the first chase sequence in Act Three, scene two, which made a hilarious picture. Yes, things look up once more.

I decided it was tactically the right moment to deal with the lazy fairy. With everyone looking out of the corners of their eyes, I asked her to leave rehearsals. She put on a brave front but she had clearly not expected to be kicked out. The story made the rounds of the theatre.

Tamara phoned from the Canadian Embassy to say that ECS had FAXed their agreement to the various terms and conditions and that the sponsorship will proceed. Now we can afford some of the electronic equipment the production desperately needs. I'm curious how Orlov will react.

I spent the evening working with the lovers. Vera Leskova has agreed to keep working with us until we find a suitable replacement for Hermia. I have promised her that she will get to play the part sometimes (when I am not there to see it). Irina as Helena has genuine child-like charm, gushing with hurt love as she tries to hold on to Demetrius in the forest, proud and vulnerable when the two men "woo her at once." And open to the audience. There is no problem in understanding why Oberon should feel touched by her plight, and want to sort out her love problems for her. Irina's danger is a tendency to whine and indulge in self-pity. Helena must avoid these obvious temptations.

We are on the road to differentiating Lysander and Demetrius, the former as the poet-intellectual, the latter as the jock hunk. So often the lovers are played as interchangeable, which is a superficial reading of the text. Andrey, as Lysander, is enjoying the chance to explore a comic portrayal of a quasi-Pushkin type, the poet who understands love through words rather than deeds. In English "Lysander" suggests the word "lie" and therefore an ability to play with words but this is lost in translation. "For lying so, Hermia I do not lie" (Act Two, scene two) is not in Russian a pun on the character's name. This, to me, is one of the reasons I must aerate some of the subtext with strong visual images. We have imagined

Lysander as the brain of the class. We've given him glasses and a little notebook in which he writes all his *bon mots*. "Demetrius" makes me hear "meat," and so we've made him the macho male kind who swaggers through the forest ceaselessly challenging Lysander to a fight. In the first scene of the play Lysander calls him a "spotted man." This is another hook on which I hang the possibility of a birthmark for Demetrius. (Except in the Russian translation the insult is different so I can't use the text to support my argument in my attempt to persuade Alexei to mark his face.) A birthmark would certainly give Helena an emotional motivation for her love: "Things base and vile, holding no quantity, / Love can transpose to form and dignity." Helena, like a true teenager, has the hubris to assume that her love can transform the "spotted" Demetrius. In addition, Elizabethan folklore attributes a birthmark on an infant to the work of fairies. And at the end of the play Demetrius is the one character left to live his life with the fairy spell still on him. Also, I naturally love the visual reference to the current leader of the Soviet Union.

Sergei is starting to have a good time with his skateboard ("skate" in Russian). He is far from adept and he's worried, with reason, about the dilapidated state of the stage floor which makes his task very difficult. I tried to give him a few homo-erotic gestures for Puck when he is about to put the spell on the sleeping Lysander. Sergei was obviously uncomfortable. He tried the pelvic thrusts gingerly and then dropped the gestures the next time we went through the scene. Puck's sexual proclivities and sense of humour should be open to all possibilities but when I asked Sergei to reinstate the thrusts he reluctantly complied. Homosexuality is still illegal in the USSR and he is nervous about the implications of his actions. He continues to thrive in the role, though, and is quite prepared otherwise to expose his personal maniacal streak.

At the end of rehearsal I was told we would be losing Lysander for the rest of my stay. He has to fly to Cuba to shoot a film. This means he will miss the stumble-through of the entire play, which two weeks ago we had scheduled for Monday to accommodate his request to leave on Tuesday. Now because of some typical fuck-up he is going a day early. I said simply that if he left before Monday's work-through then we would find another Lysander for the production. Marianna ran off in a tizzy after this announcement.

Sunday, April 22, 1990

Puck: And so far am I glad it so did sort,
  As this their jangling I esteem a sport. (Act III, scene ii)

Valera has again taken us under his wing. After a short and unprofitable rehearsal (those kids' matinées again), this gentle, generous Russian took us up to Moscow University for a perfect view of the city and the river from the Lenin Hills. Another paradox—as I like Moscow more and more, I get more and more homesick. Then he drove us south for an hour to Melichovo, Chekhov's former estate. It's an unimposing collection of small buildings: one for cooking, one for dining, one for sleeping and one in which he both practised his medicine and wrote. This tiny two-room building has a flag-pole in front. Apparently Chekhov ran the flag up to indicate to the peasants that he was available for consultation and took it down when he wanted to write. Across a field is the tiny schoolhouse he had built for the children of the peasants in the area. The estate exudes an aura of peace and order. His sister, who was a painter, ran the household for him. Now that is the life!

Driving in Valera's Lada is a risk to life and limb. One of the rear wheels wobbles and sitting in the back feels like being the laundry in an over-loaded washing machine. Back in Moscow he proudly showed us his newly renovated studio and his private-time obsessions, a collection of his own pen and ink drawings of extraordinary Daliesque visions of the world. This mild man has some very dark sides to his soul.

At the end of the day I stopped in at Tamara's to watch a Canada-Czechoslovakia hockey game from the world championships in Switzerland on her big western colour TV. Two urgent phone calls arrived, one from Mosfilm,[10] and one from the Ministry of Culture. They had heard I intended to fire Lysander if he didn't make tomorrow's work-through of the whole play. They pleaded it was not the actor's fault. The theatre had been informed when Andrey would be needed for the film but had not bothered to inform me. Was there some invisible Puck somewhere playing with my life? Was this Marianna again with her cold look? Obviously I can't blame the actor. Christ, here I go again, backing off at yet another ultimatum. How on earth did they know where I was? At least Canada won the

[10] The State-run film production company.

hockey game.[11]

Now that the sponsor is secure I intend to sit down with Orlov and draft a list of demands. I won't come back unless the theatre guarantees to meet them. I'll let the sponsorship money do some of the talking. I need access to the students full time, all the actors in rehearsal when called, and a precise production schedule for the fall.

Monday, April 23, 1990

Helena: We, Hermia, like two artificial gods,
   Have with our needles created both one flower,
   Both on one sampler, sitting on one cushion,
   Both warbling of one song, both in one key,
   As if our hands, our sides, voices, and minds,
   Had been incorporate. (Act III, scene ii)

The day of the stagger-through to permit all departments involved to grasp the scope of the play. It will provide the basis for a discussion of the work on the choreography and music that must take place while I am out of the country. Monday is the regular day off, but I had been promised the entire company for the day. Now Lysander is winging his way across the Atlantic, and neither the original Flute nor the understudy arrived for rehearsal.[12]

We carefully negotiated our way through almost the entire production, running out of time in the middle of Act Five. At each scene I would explain to Arkady or the designers or Tanya and Sergei what was missing, what we are aiming for, where the music comes in and how they should work. Despite the long day it was possible to see that the production will be an immense, varied and very rich piece of theatre. The students as the soldiers and the fairies are providing a massive influx of energy. Oleg loves his encounter with Titania and the host of nubile female fairies.

"More women," he kept crying, with a big grin on his face as more appeared to do his bidding, "more women!"

It was both the actor's and the character's idea of heaven. Russians are much freer than we are with straight sexual play in public. Both Oleg and

---

[11] The team did well in the first round of the championship but disgraced themselves in their final game against the USSR so badly they were booed by the Swiss fans.

[12] The understudy arrived later in the day with a doctor's certificate, suggesting I frame it as a souvenir of working in Russia.

Sasha think nothing of nibbling at one of Titania's very beautiful breasts in front of the other actors. They do it chastely and playfully, and Masha likes it too. When it comes to any homo-erotic gestures or any business involving their arse, however, they immediately frown and shake their heads.

Sergei and Tanya are a marvel to watch at work together. They can demonstrate a movement or dance step interchangeably, and they understand one another so well they complete each other's sentences. At one point Tanya was physically inventing a movement that would permit the fairies to throw a bolt of energy across the stage at the lovers. She made a sweeping motion with her arms and then Sergei jumped on stage and "received" the bolt with his body. He then threw it back, demonstrating a refinement of Tanya's movement. She accepted his suggestion physically and returned it to him with a further refinement. Then both of them immediately grabbed the students and started teaching the movement, exploring and creating as one spirit in two separate bodies. Just before Oberon was to make one of his entrances, all the students playing the male fairies mounted the platforms upstage. They were still jerry-rigged. There was an ugly, awful sound of splitting wood and a terrible crash. The whole group fell through the set. By some miracle no one was hurt. The technicians and the actors themselves just shrugged off the incident as though it didn't happen.

In one of the breaks I asked Arkady if the Jewish accent that Yuri was doing as Quince was offensive. Arkady's eyes flashed behind his glasses but he would not look at me. To be a Jew in the Soviet Union means to have "Jewish" stamped on one's passport as one's nationality. Arkady is Jewish.

"I realize," I explained to him, "that these are difficult times."

"Yes, of course, these are difficult times," he mumbled.

I went on, "I don't want to offend. We don't want the audience to laugh at the Georgian or the Ukrainian or the Jew in the production. The ethnic diversity is intended to be a celebration of the size and composition of the Soviet Union."

"Yes, I understand," he replied. He was still not looking at me, but finally he added quietly, "Maybe Quince's accent is a little too much. And maybe Wall's Georgian accent is a little too strong as well."

Hmm. I know I am playing with fire in trying to keep the audience laughing with and not at the characters. Surely if it is done with genuine respect, even a foreigner like myself can play with these associations? Surely an enjoyment of the ethnic cornucopia is a small drop of medicine in these difficult times?

As I came out of the theatre after this long day, Gorky Street was eerily empty. A steady drizzle had turned the asphalt into a shiny black mirror, except in the centre of the street which had been chewed up by the passage of what must have been a large number of heavy, tracked vehicles. And there they were, in Pushkin Square, a line of tanks standing silently in the rain. Soldiers stood at attention. My blood froze. There's been a military coup, I assumed. Wrong (for now, anyhow). It was merely a matter of the tanks moving to the Kremlin in preparation for the celebration of Lenin's birthday and the May Day parade.

Tuesday, April 24, 1990

Flute: And the Duke had not given him sixpence a day for playing Pyramus, I'll be hang'd. (Act IV, scene ii)

In his office, sitting in those awkward red plush chairs and surrounded by pictures of Tairov and Chekhov on the walls, I asked Yury Yeremin for his view on the future of theatre in Russia.

"There will be some changes on the artistic scene," Yury said. "People are gathering their strength before the big leap. We have to let the history of what is happening to us go through us so that we understand it. We shouldn't hurry. We need new words and new means of expression. At the moment neither the directors nor the actors nor the audience believe the words any more. The playwrights have gone silent. Even someone like Alexandr Gelman, one of our most gifted writers, isn't writing. He is in his fifth year working on a play called *Coffee and Cognac*. He can't finish it."

"Who gives you the money to run the theatre?" I asked.

"The Ministry of Culture. If we have a good year they give us less money," he said. "Our grant is small. The Moscow Art Theatre gets one and one-half million roubles a year. The Pushkin gets only one hundred thousand. We used to get more, but since we have been having a few good years we now get less. But now the Ministry is too preoccupied with the proposed move to a market economy, which is to happen on June 1st, to be interfering in the theatre, raising or lowering the grants. An army of government bureaucrats and civil servants will lose their jobs. They are expecting a million people to be unemployed. It looks like we might be pushed into a commercial theatre system, and artistic directors like myself don't want that. Serious art should not have to be commercial. The Union of Theatre Workers is taking over more and more of the running of the theatres. They are trying to introduce a system whereby every director and every actor is guaranteed a salary to work at their art no matter where they are employed. Directors have started to accept contracts at theatres rather than permanent employment to demonstrate that the new system is possible. New actors to a company are being hired on a contract basis only. Of course, for this new system to really work, the government is going to have to change their passport system so that artists can move freely from city to city."[13]

"Can you fire an actor who is a member of your permanent company?" I asked.

"If they don't break the union rules or aren't undisciplined, then they can't be fired. As soon as the actors become freelance artists under the new system then we will be able to fire them. This means we will lose the advantages of a permanent company. There is a lot to be gained from working with a nucleus of actors for six or seven years, so that everyone shares a style and vision. I hope we can find a way of combining the two systems so we have both creativity and change."

Yury is driven when he is on the subject of his own theatre. The words rush out with such volume and pace you get the sensation of being pushed back in your seat. This is how he earns the right to be the director in the rehearsal hall, this is how he subdues his actors. He has kept his distance from the *Dream* rehearsals. Is he avoiding any challenge to his status in his own space? Why has he not extended the simplest of Russian courtesy gestures and invited me to his home? Strange.

As I was coming out of Yury's office, Elena, the Stage Manager, was rushing by in a flap because the actors' pay packets had not appeared.

"We pretend to work and they pretend to pay us," she laughed as she ran off to find someone in accounting who would get the actors their money.

Too many of the actors are still pretending to work for me. How do I change this? "Don't bother trying to understand Russia," everyone keeps saying. "You just have to love her." "We Russians carry our country around

[13] At the moment you can't live in any city in the Soviet Union unless you have official permission and this is stamped in your passport.

inside us," Elena Skorokhodova warned me. "It may look like it is falling to pieces, but if some foreigner tries to take over they will learn the lesson of all past invaders."

Marianna's teen-age daughter just returned from a student exchange with a school in Belgium. She announced on her return that she didn't want to live in Russia any more. By happenstance she had been chosen to be interviewed by Belgian television and had outraged her teachers by saying about Gorbachev, "He talks a lot, but he doesn't do anything."

I fit in four hours with the mechanicals, laying the foundation for Tanya, Sergei and the actors to develop the staging of the play-within-the-play. I want to leave room for them to invent the business of the "merry tragedy" of Pyramus and Thisby themselves. They must engage their own imagination, and not be limited by my preconceptions from previous productions. Vadim Ledogorov, the original Flute, finally turned up. With a typical Russian shrug he calmly stepped back into the role. What a good actor! I tried to prepare all of them, but in particular Vadim, for the necessity of Flute's death monologue turning the "merry" into "tragedy." Puzzlement. They don't realize that the Pyramus/Thisby story will bring the house down. It was suggested that Starveling could be a Tartar. Nina actually looks like one: dark and burly and round-faced. But she angrily refused. Playing a Tartar involves an ethnic stigma she finds too distasteful to touch, even in a comedy. They all have difficulty remembering to alter "Peter Pigva" (Peter Quince) to "Pyotr Pigva." They can't believe that Russian names deserve to be in a Shakespeare play. How Canadian these Russians are.

Assia had another angina attack today. Too much greasy food. Too many cigarettes. And too much worry about the suffering she sees around her. She is going to buy Valera two new tires for his Lada as a gift.

Wednesday, April 25, 1990

Bottom: ... to say the truth, reason and love keep little company together now-a-days. (Act III, scene i)

One of the better days. A couple of hours with Sasha (Oberon) and the students trying to find the movement aesthetic that captures the feel of an urban forest-magical creature. Because Sergei and Tanya still look for clinical movements for actors rather than behaviour patterns for characters, the result is cold instead of sexual.

Assia, as is her daily habit, arrived late for rehearsals. She is now completely part of the project, frequently acting as interpreter. The actors treat her like a queen. All work stops as she walks across the stage, saying good morning to the cast and heading for her seat in the auditorium. She usually comes in dispensing gifts: cigarettes or food she bought with hard currency or an article of clothing she liberated from somewhere. Today she handed Sasha a pair of second-hand jeans scrounged from someone at the Embassy. There was a flash of anger in Sasha's eyes. For a moment he thought he was being patronized, turned into an object of western charity, and his Ukrainian pride rebelled. It took half the morning before Assia's unassuming generosity calmed him down. As librarian at the NTS for nearly twenty-five years she has seen the play produced numerous times in English, but this morning she said with real emotion: "You know, this is the first time that I understand the words. The language is beautiful!" She is always commenting on how good the translation is.

Our approach will result in a very clear telling of the story. Will it appear obvious and superficial? Shakespeare has an extraordinary ability to render the profound simple. Will all the subtleties we are developing be hidden by the strong brush strokes? Theseus is an ambiguous figure for the Russians. Modelled upon the stable, benevolent dictatorship of Elizabeth I, he is far from any example the Russians have in their recent history. But democracy took hundreds of years to develop in England, and the Soviets are expecting it to happen overnight. They are too impatient to accept the possibility that Gorbachev might have any traits of a benevolent tyrant.

Arkady is playing along in rehearsal with a very rudimentary Russian synthesizer that resembles in its capabilities the toy electric piano of a three-year-old. Every time Sasha raises his voice Arkady's instinct is to underscore it with what he thinks is horror music. We don't have the time to explore any second and third choices, and by the time I come back all the tapes will have been made. There won't be time to develop the music any further.

Fortunately, Puck will be great. This lonely demi-devil Puck with a very dark sense of humour is going to add a resonance I have never seen in any production before. While we were discussing Puck's need to relate to the audience, Oleg jumped in with: "In Russia we don't have a relationship with the audience. We have Stanislavsky. We have the fourth wall."

Again I explained that the monologues are not internal. I pointed out that Elizabethan actors had such a huge work-load that the cast for a play like *Hamlet* had an astonishingly limited number of rehearsals. They learned the lines and had to rely on their own instincts. There was no time for Stanislavskian naturalistic questions about motivation. The actors must look the audience in the eye and allow its presence to be an impetus to push deeper into the characters. There is a certain leap of faith that every Shakespearean actor must make to capture the character. I used the analogy of the stuntman who jumped from one tower of the Toronto Dominion Centre to the other this month. At some point each actor has to jump and trust that he will make it to the other side. The monologue is a performance *through* the audience to that part of the character's self we all spend a good deal of our own daily lives performing for—the "internal audience" for which we do everything from lying and dissembling eloquently to performing acts of heroism. We can be both actor and audience for our own performances. Theatre is not merely a venue where one group of humans performs for other humans. Theatre is actually a recreation of the internal structure of human nature.

I have to confess that Masha will be a good Titania after all. She loves flaunting her sexuality. Her weakness is that she isn't interested in an intellectual defence of womankind. She asked me what the difference was between Titania's feelings for Oberon and her feelings for Bottom. "Love and Lust," I answered. If we take our cue from Bottom's lines, then lust is love with the absence of reason.

I finally found the perfect Hermia! A young girl just out of theatre school who will give us a perfect spoiled rich-kid character to complement the work of the three other young actors. Yury is going to hire her for his company. She will one day be a formidable actress.

Saturday, April 28, 1990

Quince: ... I am to entreat you, request you, and desire you, to con them by to-morrow night; (Act I, scene ii)

I'm sitting in the airport, having once again "escaped" through Customs, Immigration and the interminable line-ups of a Soviet airport. As I wait for my flight to be called I'm trying to recreate the final encounter with the full cast earlier in the day. At a brief meeting in which I laid out my ultimatums for better organization and co-operation in the fall, Orlov nodded from behind his ubiquitous cloud of smoke with great conviction. Then I joined the cast in the auditorium. They listened patiently as I explained that in these past four weeks we had not achieved nearly as much as I had hoped. I said that over the summer they must learn their lines as quickly as possible, and work with Andrey (the Assistant Director) to maintain the blocking as we had worked it out with Tanya and Sergei. They nodded solemnly. Once again I asked them to remember how important the words are with Shakespeare. They were not to add, subtract, modernize, improvise or improve on the text in any way. The characters in the court particularly must work for a classical, traditional delivery. Quince in Act Five can easily show us what happens if an actor doesn't observe the punctuation or the ends of lines. "Our true intent is all for your delight / We are not here that you should here repent you" can with improper pauses become "All for your delight we are not here."

I asked if there were any questions. Dead silence. This made me furious. Adding some moral indignation to my voice, after first apologizing for my presumptuousness, I gave them shit for their working methods and general lack of respect for theatre itself. I explained that theatre should be sacred to us, should be cared for with our soul, or else we should find another job. I said I had been amazed by their laziness and sloppiness. I had come to Russia thinking I would find in theatre the same discipline and work ethic you can find in Russian hockey, ballet and the circus. Instead, I found disinterest, apathy and a lack of imagination and focus. By now my voice was riding a fair amount of anger. No questions! Why aren't they curious about Shakespeare, why don't they ask about the text, the concept, Elizabethan acting? The only question anyone at the Pushkin ever asks is, "Am I free to go now?"

The actors sat glumly in their seats when I had finished. Sergei and Tanya, true workaholics, of course agreed with what I had said but they were glum anyway. It spoiled the leave-taking for those actors with whom I was enjoying working. Alone in one seat, unknown to the cast, with the excitement of an actor who has just landed her first professional job, sat Maria Andreeva, the new Hermia. Valera sent us off with moist eyes and a couple of his drawings as gifts. I had a vague inkling I would soon be desperate to come back and start work again.

* * *

If you fly Swissair from Moscow to Toronto you have to stay overnight in Zurich. They put you up free of charge in the Novotel, at the airport, a cleaner and more antiseptic version of every airport hotel you have ever stayed in. The first thing I did when I got to my room was to open every piece of luggage and take out every article of clothing and item, and spread them around the room. I suspected I was carrying some Moscow stowaways. Sure enough, as I was shaving that night a little brown creature scuttled across the sink. I managed to swat it. The next morning as I was having my bath, there was another one running along the side of the tub. I swatted and missed. It zipped under the bath and disappeared. While I can happily say that no little six-legged Muscovites seem to have made it back to Toronto, I cannot suppress a little chuckle at the possibility that the Zurich Novotel is unwitting home to a family of immigrant Russian cockroaches.

SECOND INTERMISSION

Returning home was an immediate plunge back into the icy morass of the Canadian Stage. Within days I was on a retreat in a Kawartha log cabin with my new producer, my new production manager and a handful of production personnel, forging a team that could handle the tough financial road ahead with clarity and motivation. This new team represented the culmination of the transition from a group that had worked with Bill Glassco to one that could work with me. Now we only had to wait for the board to deal with the problem of the General Manager and then reorganize the administration to properly support the work on the stage, and we would have a company capable of fighting for the mandate of our theatre in a political environment increasingly hostile to Canadian artistic endeavours.

At the beginning of June, the Pushkin Theatre was in Quebec City as part of La Quinzaine Internationale du Théâtre with their adaptation of a Chekhov short story, *Ward Six*. I'd spoken to Sasha and Valera over the phone and was wondering how to find the time to squeeze in a drive to see them. So successful had their production been that the festival had had to add performances to accommodate the audiences. The combined pleasure of a Chekhov in Russian and a vernal Quebec City was, alas, one that I had to forgo this particular June.

At ten-thirty on the night of June 4th the hollow ring of two pairs of feet on the metal stairs leading up to my office sounded the knell of the Canadian Stage's future. Jim Leech, the President of the board of the theatre, had come, as arranged, to report on the outcome of the board meeting that had just finished. That he brought David Black with him was an immediate signal that the news was going to be disastrous. David is a friend. He had been President of the Toronto Free Theatre's board and together we had provided the city with a great deal of exciting theatre. He had obviously been brought along to soften the blow.

The board, Jim informed me, had decided the theatre needed "a change of leadership." They had looked at the cash flow projections for the season that they had accepted back in January and announced in March, and concluded that unless they acted now the theatre would have to close its doors by October. The only hope for survival, the board felt, was to "chop off my head," as Jim put it, and to go begging to the funding agencies for bail-out money, stating, "Look, we have made a fresh start. Save us." Bob Baker was to be the new Artistic Director and Bill Glassco was coming back to help with the transition.

As I sat there and listened to Jim, with his boyish looks and over-eager charm, profess his admiration for my work as an artist—he even managed to say with seeming conviction that he loved me—a big black void spread through my gut. I cursed my naïveté in not seeing it coming. I cursed my belief in the necessity of founding the Canadian Stage in the first place. I cursed the misplaced hubris that had me believing my shoulders were big enough to carry on against impossible odds and despite the handicaps and shackles imposed by the board. I cursed the time wasted propping up Bill Glassco during his two years as Producing Artistic Director of the company. Somehow I held on to myself.

Poor David. As lawyer, he was squirming with pain inside his Bay Street suit, caught between the boys from Tridel, Imperial Oil and *Toronto Life,* and his human self which was profoundly aware of both the wrongness and injustice of the decision. He hung his head, unable to look at me. On the walls around us were photographs and posters from past victories in the struggle to create theatre. R.H. Thomson as Hamlet. *Jungle of the Cities. Translations.* In the corner sat a beautiful model of the proposed new innovative performance space for the site. A feasibility study had come up with a design concept but we hadn't been able to move into the fundraising or construction phase. On my desk sat a small framed reproduction of an Hieronymus Bosch painting entitled *Judgement Day.* It depicts angels carrying mortals up to what looks like a giant tube in the sky. I had inscribed next to the painting, "One day the Artistic Directors of the world will be delivered to the great sewer pipe in the sky."

I expressed my outrage that I had not been allowed to address the board and insisted I be given the opportunity. Jim said he would have to think about that and went off to consult Peter Herndorff on the matter.

PHOTOS

from rehearsals and the production of
A Midsummer Night's Dream

Oberon

Puck

Oberon and Puck

Helena and Hermia

Student fairies

Titania and fairies

Hermia and Theseus

Bottom

Bottom before we cut his cowboy hat

Bottom on the goddamn vehicle. Note ECS.

A truly Russian Bottom with balalaika singing "The Ousel Cock."

Bottom with his harem

"for aught that I could ever read, ...
The course of true love never did run smooth." (Act I, scene i)

Snug to Quince: "Have you the lion's part written? Pray you, if it be,
give it me, for I am slow of study" (Act I, scene ii)

Titania in rehearsal. "Therefore the moon (the governess of floods),
Pale in her anger, washes all the air," (Act II, scene i)

Hermia and Lysander in Tanya and Sergei's boxing ring (Act III, scene ii)

Demetrius and Lysander worshipping Helena (Act III, scene ii)

The Mechanicals' band. Note Snug's Kruschev makeup
which we discarded after one preview.

A Georgian bricklayer as Wall

The incident with the glasses (Act V, scene i)

The director explaining some of the finer points of being an ass

Curtain call

He eventually phoned to offer me the chance to talk to the executive the next day. This was clearly a sop and I didn't bother with it, insisting instead on addressing the full board. Finally, on Wednesday, two days later, I was permitted to speak at a board meeting attended by eighteen of the forty-five board members who cared enough about the theatre to show up. In the meantime Jim Leech issued a press release on the matter. The hijacking was a *fait accompli*. My performance on that Wednesday will not rank as one of the high points of my public speaking career.

As days and then weeks went by, the extent of the manipulation and misinformation that had preceded the hijacking of the Canadian Stage became evident. The review committee with which I had met on seemingly amicable terms to discuss the artistic future of the theatre[1] had become while I was out of the country a performance review of my one year as Producing Artistic Director. Under the guise of consulting the theatre community about the role Canadian Stage should have, they had talked to a small number of people and then distorted their opinions and statements in a "report" that was then put to the board—a manipulation that Richard Rose,[2] for one, vilified in a public letter. It was also implied to the board that the major funding bodies were going to start cutting back on their grants if a change was not made. This was a patent fabrication. The Canada Council had in fact just recommended the first increase in years on the basis of the proposed season.

The review committee's report was shoddy and riddled with inaccuracies and, according to actor Tom Butler, who was on the board at the time, the executive did not even provide adequate time for the board members to read the document before they were asked to vote on it. Over nine years I had contributed more than my share to both the Toronto Free Theatre and to the formation of the Canadian Stage. That I had not been given a real opportunity to address the allegations in the review committee's report was a miscarriage of justice of gargantuan proportions. It was of course no mere accident. If I had been allowed to explain the origin of the chaos at the theatre some of the clearer heads on the board might have realized what was going on. David Black later explained to me he thought the reason the board did not discuss dismissing the General Manager by herself was that this would make the board member who chaired the search committee that found her look like he had made a bad mistake.

[1] See page 27.
[2] Artistic Director of Necessary Angel Theatre Company, and one of Canada's most respected theatre directors.

When the board's press release appeared it managed to infer I was being replaced because I was responsible for a huge accumulated deficit. Nothing could be further from the truth. Glassco had run up over two million in operating losses over CanStage's first two seasons. I had inherited this legacy. While my first season was also going to rack up an operating loss, it would have been the smallest in the three-year history of the new organization. Of course, with artists contracted, sets built and marketing material printed, changing the playbill was a financial disaster, worse even than any doomsday scenario for the all-Canadian season.[3] Enough.

Why would a major arts organization behave this way? If they had simply wanted to get rid of me they could have just let my contract run out; it had only one more year to go. This would have done a great deal less harm to me personally and, more importantly, it would have been a great deal less harmful for the theatre in the long run. It seemed the board just couldn't resist the *frisson* of Bay Street executive executions. Jim Leech is the President of Unicorp Canada and in the happier times of the mid-80s he snatched Union Gas in a takeover battle that earned him great Bay Street reviews as a corporate raider. Unicorp shares, in the twelve months previous to my firing, had plummeted and the value of the corporation had dropped one hundred million dollars on the Toronto Stock Exchange.

What a long way since the early '70s when theatre spaces were built from converted warehouses with the sweat of underpaid artists and administrators. The evolution of artistic groups into corporate organizations in which artists themselves have little say and no control is the result of a number of clear historical forces. To qualify for the special tax status of a charity, most theatres are legally set up as corporations without share capital. This means they must have members who elect directors under by-laws that are usually borrowed from standard corporate practice. But in many ways Canadian theatre is a victim of its own aspirations and the perceived necessity of cosying up to the conservative corporate culture of the '80s. Canadian theatre, rightly or wrongly, in the middle of the last decade developed an intense desire to free itself from the ghettoization of small theatre spaces and capture the citadel of the mainstream with pride and confidence. The Canadian Stage itself was founded with that primary purpose. Big Canadian plays in a big theatre produced by a big company for big audiences. No longer would the public be permitted to see the works

---

[3] The financial statements for the year ending June 30th, 1990 allow for a write-off of $434,000 against the disaster. A full accounting of the fiasco might almost double that figure. Not a financially responsible use of tax-payers' money!

of Shakespeare or Shaw as the most important theatre we can stage. Our own plays produced to perfection would be the engine that helped drive the next phase of our theatre exploration and development. We had to have bigger budgets to reach wider audiences and to do this, of course, we had to sell our soul to the great gods Marketing and Fund-raising. We needed to build up vast fund-raising departments to organize and execute expensive campaigns. No longer was it sufficient for theatre workers to define and control their marketing strategies. We needed experts. Onto the boards of our organizations came the corporate presidents of advertising agencies to show the theatre amateurs how it is done. The actual work, the plays themselves, became less and less the focus as the value of the packaging increased.

The '80s were the era of shrinking government contributions to the arts. The Canada Council claims that in the last four years alone the buying power of its grants has shrunk by twenty percent. This is part of a Conservative agenda in Ottawa to make the arts less dependent upon government and more "self-sufficient." Inevitably, the arts have become more dependent on corporate donations and sponsorship. Now arts organizations are out on the hunt for senior executives of major corporations to put on their boards. "We'll trade you the kudos of being an arts patron if you throw a little donation or sponsorship our way once a year." For a sum that might in rare cases make up five percent of the total cost of a production, as a sponsor a corporation is able to place its logo on all associated publicity and claim publicly a kind of ownership of that production. (And most often also be able to claim this donation as a tax deduction!) In effect, grants to an arts organization (our taxes) and the work of the underpaid artists (their personal subsidies) have been co-opted by an oil company, a brewery or an insurance company.

The financial distress of our arts organizations has thus had a huge influence on the composition of all boards in this country. A corporate board was seen as the saviour of a cash-strapped theatre like CanStage. We now have advertising executives mingling with CEOs and executive VPs of companies such as Imperial Oil, Molson's and Tridel. Add the management consultants and accountants desperate to network with and impress these same people at board meetings with their adroit analyses or innovative financial packages, factor in would-be cultural moguls like the publisher of *Toronto Life* magazine, and you have an ungainly mess, a disaster looking to happen.

Meanwhile the artists were legally barred from being involved in the running of their own organizations. In 1987 the Supreme Court of Ontario, in a decision involving the Ontario Humane Society, ruled that no one who is actually employed by a non-profit organization may sit on its board. This has been effectively used to keep artists off the boards of larger organizations. I was always a member of the Toronto Free Theatre board, for instance, but when the merger that formed Canadian Stage took place I was told I could not be a member of the new organization because of the Supreme Court ruling. Ironically, if I had been a member of the board I would have been better protected than I was as the Artistic Director. In most corporate by-laws, as a matter of respect for the dignity of the businessman, it takes a vote of two-thirds of the *entire* board to dismiss a board member, whereas for the artist, as in the case of the CanStage hijacking, it was sufficient to have less than fifty percent of the board vote for the dismissal.

How do we begin to assess how the conservative nature of our board structures has affected the selection and execution of our work? What is the constant kowtowing to the corporate world doing to the self-confidence of our artists?

Somewhere in the great beyond, Tairov, I knew, understood what I was going through. Over the course of the summer, entertainment sections of the newspapers had a field day as board members resigned publicly (David Black was one of the board members who resigned) and artistic associations such as Actors' Equity, Playwrights Union of Canada and the Professional Association of Canadian Theatres all struggled valiantly to try to find a public position on such a volatile issue. Then the cast of *The Comedy of Errors*, the show in High Park which, to no one's surprise, I now declined to direct, held a virtual sit-in at the theatre during the first week of rehearsals in reaction to the fiasco. I urged them to carry on with the production despite everything because I was very worried that if High Park was cancelled for one summer it might mean the end of theatre there for good. After fighting the board for three years to keep the "Dream in High Park," I didn't want to see it disappear now. Director Peter Hinton, in an act of courage and generosity, agreed to take on the cast and the designs and the basic concept for the show, and complete the staging. In addition, Susan Serran, former Artistic Director of Theatre Direct, and Jerry Doiron, the General Manager of Necessary Angel, determined that more was at stake than my somewhat acerbic nature and spent a great deal of their time trying to bring a public focus onto the issue of who should be running our artistic organizations, and drafted a public letter signed by about one hundred leading members of the theatre community. Chris Newton showed true character in publicly attacking the actions of CanStage's board, thereby risking the ire of his own. He had recognized the importance of the principles involved.

In the '90s, along with the big questions such as how the pieces of the Canadian conundrum might fit together without Quebec, we artists have to sort through the problems of the structuring and the nurturing of our artistic organizations.

Throughout the long and painful summer, Moscow kept flitting through my mind. Obviously I was due to have a long chat with Tairov, but I was also desperate just to get away from the crisis and back to my *métier.*

* * *

Like a deep-sea diver who must pause on the way down to allow his/her body to become accustomed to the increased pressure, I needed a brief stop in Berlin on my way back to Moscow at the beginning of October. The two former halves of the city are like two unequal Siamese twins, one healthy and one withered. Bicycling for hours through the city as it prepared for the unification celebrations left me with an ugly foretaste of the years of unimaginable emotional grief that are to come. It was the last day for Poles and Czechs to legally enter the former East Germany without a visa. The eastern "hordes" had invaded the shops of West Berlin and were carrying off every cheap electronic device available. The downtown intersections were clogged with cartons and cases of televisions and stereos being shlepped, dollied or dragged back to the kilometre after kilometre of chartered buses parked along the boulevard leading to the Brandenburg Gate. Would western materialist society have the wisdom to recognize anything of value in the defeated East? Already the police in the former eastern sector were outfitted rather awkwardly in western uniforms. On stand-by for the projected crowds for that evening's celebrations, the dilapidated, ancient ambulances from the former "Democratic" Republic stood humiliated next to the shiny, latest model Mercedes Benz ambulances of the "Federal" Republic. What used to be a frustrating twenty- or thirty-minute passport inspection at S-BAHN Friedrichstrasse to see a production by Brecht's Berliner Ensemble is now a thirty-second skip down a flight of stairs. But the Berlin theatre community is buzzing with rumours of wholesale shut-downs of the erstwhile eastern theatres. Now that the city is one, it is presumed that half the total number of theatres will be superfluous.

The former East Berlin is very like Moscow. Dirty, drab, smelling of coal-fired electricity plants, and with the same pot-holes in the roads. At midnight of October 3rd I stood on Unter den Linden, not fifty yards from the university where my parents had met, crushed in a crowd of a million Germans partying at the official rebirth of "one Fatherland." They were understandably overjoyed yet too embarrassed to let it out. With the television cameras of the world trained on them, the Germans were determined not to gloat too outrageously over having annexed a slice of eastern Europe. It was the best-behaved crowd of one million imaginable, watching the fireworks in silence. The evening was a non-event.

The work of the Schaubuehne seemed to have temporarily hit some kind of dead zone. This extraordinary theatre, run in a unique way by the artists themselves as a temple of theatrical research, development and experimentation, was for the first time in my experience only one third full. Stein's latest production, Bernard-Marie Koltès's *Roberto Zucco*, had the usual detailed extravagance, but was an irrelevancy in the whirligig of history outside the theatre's doors.

In a small bookstore I found a rare copy of Tairov's book on theatre, a monograph written in the early '20s called *Notes of a Director*, though the title in German translates as *Theatre Unbound*. Sitting in my seat on the Aeroflot flight to Moscow from the former East Berlin airport, with a dooser of a cold, and flying first class so that I could put the DX7 synthesizer I was bringing as a gift to the Pushkin in the empty seat next to me,[4] I hunkered down and started to read Tairov's thoughts. The founder of the theatre I was working in and I have very different ideas on what theatre should be. Would he understand and be sympathetic to what I was trying to do?

---

[4] I didn't trust the baggage-handlers in Moscow. One month earlier they had plundered the luggage of the Montreal Canadiens.

THIRD PERIOD
Rehearsals, October 1990

Saturday, October 6, 1990

Titania: Therefore the winds, piping to us in vain,
*   As in revenge, have suck'd up from the sea*
*   Contagious fogs; which, falling in the land,*
*   Hath every pelting river made so proud*
*   That they have overborne their continents.*
*   The ox hath therefore stretch'd his yoke in vain,*
*   The ploughman lost his sweat, and the green corn*
*   Hath rotted ere his youth attain'd a beard. (Act II, scene i)*

Day one in Moscow. As I nervously dragged myself over to Customs, laden down with microphones and computerized drum machines and the synthesizer, I wondered if they might arrest me for attempted smuggling. A weary Customs officer just looked at my visa and waved me past in total boredom, not even bothering to lift his head to look at my luggage. I fought desperately to hide a big grin. There was Marianna, prim as ever. Did I detect a look of desperation in her face? The new driver is a bright-faced young man. The rain was coming down in sheets and apparently had been for months. The Lada's feeble windshield wipers couldn't handle the downpour. Igor, the driver, hit every water-filled pot-hole with abandon. The mud in the fields was so bad the tractors were useless and there in the fields, as the photographs in the *Toronto Star* had shown, was the military helping with the harvest.

Marianna confirmed there was no food in the stores. "No milk, no cheese, no nothing."

They are living a very different life from what they lived five months ago.

Once again the theatre has asked one of the administrators to vacate her apartment so that I have a place to live during my stay. She is heading off to the Caucasus on holiday in a few days. No cockroaches! Larisa (my landlady) even found a bottle of vodka somewhere which she left for me. I immediately phoned Valera and he insisted I come over. He was in a mood I didn't recognize. With his beard, his face, which had shrunk since April, his blazing eyes and his knobbly hands, and surrounded by an aura of incredible sadness, he looked like some old Russian icon. "*Vsyo normalne,*" was his constant phrase. "Everything is normal." With great embarrass-ment he and his wife Natasha laid a meagre offering of food on the table: some dry bread, the left-overs of what looked like the Russian equivalent of Spam, some fish that looked lethal, a few potatoes and some butter. I was too shocked to eat much. Valera, good diplomat that he is, tried to paint a happy picture of the progress of the set-building and the rehearsals. (They brought their teen-age son to the table to do the translating.)

As the evening wore on, he became more honest. "Since you were last here everyone has become old," he stated simply. "We don't know what we are going to do. We don't know how we can live this way." Their eyes lit up when they talked about their summer. Thanks to Assia's gift of two new wheels, their Lada had made it as far as Holland. But the summer was a long time ago.

"Nothing of the past remains, and there is nothing in the future." Valera launched into a long monologue on the glories of Russia past. "At the beginning of the century Russia had more culture, more intelligence and more wisdom than Germany, France and America put together and now there is nothing left."

Valera and Natasha, who is a director, sat side by side with the kind of comfort and understanding one doesn't often see in couples in North America. Theirs is the model Soviet family, with only one child for whom all has been sacrificed. They beamed with pride at his language skills.

Sunday, October 7, 1990

Titania: And this same progeny of evils comes
From our debate, from our dissension;
We are their parents and original. (Act II, scene i)

Igor, the new driver, is young, game, eager. An eager Igor. As I walked into the Pushkin, the ancient receptionist, who in April had been very cool and reserved, almost jumped through the glass partition to greet me. Then I bumped into one of the technicians who had never acknowledged my existence before and he too grinned and shook my hand furiously in welcome. Has something changed at the theatre? With a big smile I plunked all my electronic loot on the table in Orlov's office. His head bobbed up and down in appreciation. He made me a cup of coffee and when we were alone, I reached into my trousers and from a thigh belt loaned to me by the actor R.H. Thomson I pulled out the balance of the sponsorship in Canadian cash and plonked it with glee on the table. Orlov flicked his eyes briefly over the cash and looked back at me as if the money didn't exist. On the table was a donation that would fetch two hundred thousand roubles on the black market, two years of his theatre's entire budget, and the rhythm of his cigarette puffs hadn't altered by a nanosecond. I wouldn't want to play poker with this guy. At this point the ever curious Marianna re-entered the room unannounced. Orlov merely pulled a sheet of paper over the money and kept on talking. I reminded him of the sponsor's important requirements—a reception, the size of the company logo on the poster, etc.—and then left him to contemplate how best to use this hedge against the troubled financial future of the Pushkin.

Then with Marianna and Andrey, the Assistant Director, I tried to ascertain how much work had really been done over the summer. It seems that Tanya and Sergei have been very energetic and persistent, but we have lost three more actors. Oleg (Bottom) has left the company to follow his private production of *The Cherry Orchard* to Leningrad and elsewhere, the good Flute (Vadim Lodogorov) has decided to stay at his film school and the wonderful, crotchety actor playing old Snout is ill. Marianna and Andrey kept urging me to accept the changes: "This is life in the theatre." They assured me that I would be *spokoinyi* ("tranquil/happy") when I saw how far the cast has come in rehearsals. I'm stymied. I know these replacements mean a real watering down of the quality of the cast and the production. What do I do?

The Pushkin has a nice practice of printing a monthly performance schedule in a little booklet that is handed out to each actor. When Marianna gave me mine I opened it to the end of the month and my heart stopped when I saw, scheduled on October 30th for all to see, a preview of *A Midsummer Night's Dream*. It is actually going to happen! As we agreed in the spring they have closed the theatre down for one whole week to permit the technical rehearsals to continue without interruption. There is a buzz around the city about the show.

I went to supper at the Maly Theatre Club Restaurant (extraordinarily expensive—two hundred dollars per person at the official exchange rate) with an artist who was in Toronto over the summer. Her husband is a doctor involved in a co-operative that sells medicine. Apparently this is merely a front for a rather shady scheme to import videos and televisions from the west. Her husband had finally met the head of the co-operative at a recent meeting. Dressed in a cowboy hat and boots and accompanied by two cowboy bodyguards, he entered the room, placed his .45 on the table and announced that he was ready to do business. Gangsters are the disease of Moscow. *The Return of the Magnificent Seven* was a hit movie in Moscow and now all the gangsters imitate the Wild West. The number one topic of conversation at all the parties in the city at the moment is what kind of a gun to buy to protect oneself. Moscow will soon be able to boast that it has caught up with New York. While still in Canada I'd heard indirectly that the situation in the streets of Moscow was becoming very dangerous, for foreigners in particular, who are being mugged because food can only be securely purchased with hard currency. Meanwhile every ordinary Muscovite must help with the potato harvest out in the rain-soaked fields. Each citizen is permitted to keep one-tenth of what he or she digs up. I wonder whether Titania's "progeny of evils" speech will have any more resonance for the audience because of the weather?

Then Arkady Serper and I went through the music and discussed rehearsals. He has written some harder melodies for the fairies. We also have forty hours of studio time available if we want to re-record anything. The head sound technician grinned from ear to ear when he saw his new equipment. As we were talking, one of the theatre's administrators, an old, white-bearded, hunchbacked man with a cigar perpetually hanging out of his mouth, pushed his way through the crowd of technicians, shoved

Arkady aside and stuck out his hand. "Welcome, Guy!" This was a man I had hardly exchanged a nod with in April. Then, after telling me to meet him at ten the next morning to have my passport registered with the authorities, he turned on his heels and just as abruptly left. There is a very different attitude to the production in the corridors of the theatre.

Finally, another quick session with Marianna and Andrey, trying to sort out when the students are available for rehearsals. The three of us formed a bond to press every last possible second out of rehearsals over the next four weeks. When I came back to the apartment my landlady poured me a full glass of vodka laced with black pepper, wrapped me in wool blankets, and told me to sit with my feet in a bath of scalding hot water and then to go straight to bed. "That's the Russian way to kill a cold," she explained. Having done that, and despite this murderous bug, I can't sleep. I am too fired up.

Monday, October 8, 1990

Flute: If he [Bottom] come not, then the play is marr'd. It goes not forward, doth it?
Quince: It is not possible. You have not a man in all Athens able to discharge Pyramus but he. (Act IV, scene ii)

Marianna was asked to find a telephone number for Oleg Belkin, one of the actors from Vassiliev's company who had befriended Assia while they were in Montreal. I suspected he might be a Bottom and I wanted to audition him. Then I sat in the auditorium while Valera had the tech crew demonstrate the state of the set on the stage. What a shock! The court had not one iota of reality about it. The pillars and the scenery hung cock-eyed and looked like they were made out of cardboard, and everything was shiny metallic, in a way the forest is intended to be. It certainly didn't resemble an extension of the theatre itself. Valera sensed my horror and the atmosphere immediately got tense. He mumbled something about, "This is our life" ("*Eta nasha shizn*"). I asked him if we could change some of the paint and the decoration on the pillars so they were a direct imitation of the pillars in the auditorium. He agreed to try to make this happen. Then we looked at the forest. If anything, this was worse. Nothing but rags hanging with a few miniscule pieces of shiny metal stuck on them. The

most unimaginative and simplistic concept for a forest. The strong point of
the set is definitely not the design at the moment but the layout, which will
give the actors focus and power. When the session was over Valera shrugged
his shoulders sadly and looked away. The lighting will have to hide a great
deal.

The sound department has promised that the DX7 will be hooked up
by tomorrow. Arkady is looking forward with uninhibited eagerness to
using it. "A DX7, oh, yes, the film studio has one."

The theatre has hired a new interpreter, Helen Pirogova, to help with
rehearsals. She is an intriguing young woman with a very Russian face
behind thick glasses, buttons nicely undone down her blouse and a charm-
ingly arrogant demeanour. Normally she works for foreign businessmen
and, judging from her elegant western clothes, she is used to having money
lavished on her. She is also a top-notch, efficient interpreter, as was clear
when Oleg Belkin arrived, having been located and summoned by Marianna.
Belkin has Oleg Antonov's size, perhaps a little more intelligence and
certainly more of a sense of humour. He would make a great Bottom.
When I asked him if he would like to do the part, his eyes clouded over.
He is rehearsing for the next few months with Vassiliev, and he is not sure
if he can get permission to take time off. Vassiliev is currently one of the
most internationally fêted of Russian directors. He has long hair like Rasputin,
but runs his company like Ivan the Terrible, keeping his actors slaving away
from dawn till dusk for a pittance. Oleg has been with him for eight years
and still has no apartment, few clothes and no personal life. He was clearly
desperate for the part of Bottom, but was too terrified to ask Vassiliev's
permission. He was torn between the possibility of a big break in a respected company and the wrath of his mentor. I offered to ask Vassiliev
myself.

At supper Helen, with her air of sophistication and her perfectly applied pink lipstick, expounded on her disdain for anything Russian. "I
refuse to smoke Russian cigarettes. I want only the best. I'm spoiled." She
had just finished interpreting for a Belgian company at one hundred and
twenty dollars a day and now had consented to work for the Pushkin at
twenty-five roubles a day (five dollars) because the job looked interesting.
"I don't need politics, I don't care about politics. I don't have any influence, so why should I bother?" When we got up to leave for the offices of
Vassiliev's theatre, she insisted on paying for half of the meal.

I had met Vassiliev briefly on my first visit to Russia and in recent years the stories of his tyrannical behaviour became legion. With money earned on its many successful tours in the west, the theatre company had spectacularly renovated two floors of an old Russian building for its administrative and rehearsal home. When we arrived the place was a beehive of activity. An improv class of some kind seemed to be going on. Vassiliev himself was nowhere to be seen. None of the actors or assistants was eager to bring us to the presence of the Great One. Finally we persuaded a stage manager to take us to where he was working. As if leading us to the lair of a dragon, the fellow tiptoed up a flight of stairs and along a corridor of offices until, stopping in front of one, he motioned that this was where the master was to be found. Then he ran off to make sure he wasn't around when the door was opened. I knocked.

"Come in," came a voice from inside the room.

I opened the door and quickly threw out, "Excuse me, Anatoly, for interrupting. I am from Canada."

"Good, good," came his puzzled reply. "Come in."

Helen was hovering by the door. I motioned for her to enter. "My interpreter," I explained.

We sat down. Spread out on a table in front of him was a script he was working on. At his side the eyes of a young, dumpy assistant were popping out of her head in panic at what the great man might do as a consequence of this intrusion. I explained we had met before and I had a favour to ask him. Then I went through a pre-scripted spiel.

"I'm a foreign director trying to direct a production in this city. I've just lost one of my leads, and of course I don't know the actors of this city, but I have met Belkin and I know he would be a fabulous replacement. I have been told that the Vassiliev company will not be performing for months and I am sure that understanding my situation you will try to help me out. It would mean sparing him for only a short rehearsal period and after that a couple of nights a week." Etc. etc.

He listened and nodded with absolute impassivity, but not hostility. For a moment I thought I might have a chance. When I finished he simply stated: "I'm sorry, I can't help you. I don't like the Pushkin Theatre. I don't like those actors. Oleg has been with us for years and I wouldn't want him to work anywhere else and pick up bad habits."

I thought that his refusal was quite classy, even though granting the request would have benefitted both the pocketbook and the morale of one of the actors in his company. Vassiliev offered to come up with a list of other actors whom I should see for the part (he never did). We beat a hasty retreat.

Oleg phoned late tonight to find out what had happened. I told him that the great god Vassiliev had said "No." There was a disappointed silence at the other end. Then, believing it was Oleg's right to make his own decision, and summoning my best Russian, I offered to supplement his income in roubles from the Pushkin with Canadian dollars under the table if he played the part. There wasn't even a split-second pause. He thanked me profusely for my offer but said he was not free to accept it because he had a binding contract with Vassiliev and he had no idea what was going to happen to theatre in Russia—how many theatres might close and so forth. He didn't want to rock the boat. Wishing me a good night, he rang off.[1] As I was falling asleep I realized that should I begin to behave more like a Vassiliev, the actors might be more comfortable with me.

Tuesday, October 9, 1990

Puck: A crew of patches, rude mechanicals, ...
Were met together to rehearse a play (Act III, scene ii)

The first day of rehearsal. The entire company, including the students, was called for ten a.m. I had put Tanya in charge of organizing a stumble-through to show me the state of "the art." She elected to begin with Act Three to demonstrate what they had conceived for the movement in the forest. It was twenty-five minutes after the hour before the actors had all arrived and were ready to begin. Most of the work was horrendous. The mechanicals were a hodgepodge of phoniness; the Pyramus/Thisby play was without substance; Theseus was lazy and incomprehensible, Hippolyta confused; Puck seemed petrified of his own work and was taking nothing to the audience; Helena had been allowed to travel along the path toward whininess (why do all Helenas end up whining?). However, Tanya and Sergei had devised some very imaginative movement for the fairies and the lovers in the forest. The students were flashing back flips and pirouettes all over the place. Lysander and Demetrius looked promising, and the new

---

[1] Within three months Oleg Belkin had left the company, citing "irreconcilable differences."

Hermia is fabulous. She sticks her tits out and pouts like a true spoiled princess. In scene two of Act Three Tanya and Sergei have created a boxing ring which the fairies erect as they watch the lovers fight it out. A stroke of genius. I had to admit to myself that Vasilij Funtikov, the replacement Bottom, had more potential for the role than I imagined he would have.

After three hours I was in a state. Where do I start? The atmosphere was strained. None of the actors had come out to greet me beforehand, not even Sasha. I realized half-way through they were all afraid of what I might think about the work (especially the three new actors who had been cast over the summer) and they were shying away. When the run-through was over I asked them all to sit in the auditorium, greeting each one formally. (I was furious when I found out that administration had let some of the actors go home without my permission.) Then came the ubiquitous pep-talk.

"Thank you all for the work you have done so far. It is good but there is a very long way to go. Now, if we are to pull this off, I need every iota of your minds and your hearts to be here with me in this theatre." Again that puzzling hush fell over the cast.

After a short break we jumped straight into Egeus's entrance in the first scene. How do I get Barinov's Theseus to respond more significantly to notes encouraging him to speak out more, to be more "imperial"? This is the exact problem I had left him with in April. Valery listens nicely to me with an exaggerated seriousness and gives a little nod at the end. He then moves in his acting only a few inches in the direction I have asked him to go, just enough to show he has listened but never enough to make any kind of a breakthrough. Barinov is a fine actor, one of the leading actors of the company. His obtuseness is really frustrating. It would take so little effort on his part to actually achieve what I am after. At least we found a nice journey through the scene for Hermia. She stamps her foot when her father leaves the room and then with no warning bursts into tears as if someone had turned on a tap. Lysander's poet figure has developed into a young man totally out of touch with reality. Hermia responds with her whole being to every line he utters. With iron resolution she determines that if it is the lot of true lovers to suffer, then the two of them must suffer. When Lysander suggests they elope, banging her hand on her heart and then holding her fist up high like some adolescent imitation of a freedom fighter, she swears to be true in her love. "By Cupid's strongest bow."

After supper I once again sat down with Marianna and Andrey to try to sort out some organizational principles for rehearsals. Actors not allowed to leave unless I say so, musicians there for rehearsals, etc. Elementary stuff, but not happening at the moment.

After supper Irina Biakova tackled Helena's "How lucky some o'er other some can be" monologue at the end of the first scene. The thought process through the speech cannot be traced rationally. Helena jumps from one emotional island to the next and the connection between the two islands can be found only if you have actually inhabited the female, youthful, illogical imagination of Helena herself. Irina managed to find some of those emotional synapses. When she allows herself to explore by instinct rather than reason she can do a Helena. She has a unique way of jumping out of the play and lecturing the audience on love with real adolescent presumption.

Then Sergei worked with the "My mistress with a monster is in love" monologue. Like something out of commedia dell'arte, this monologue could almost be a comic turn, a signature piece for the actor playing Puck. I had deliberately chosen to try to make contact with Sergei on his own, to see what state he is in. His obstreperousness and his vulnerability are closely connected and he didn't take too kindly to the notes to be more sexually explicit in his actions. Nor does he ever do anything twice the same way. He is going to be a tough nut to crack.

Finally, with Masha we took a look at Titania's long "Forgeries of jealousy" speech. I explained that if she wants to avoid sentimentality she must summon concrete images in her mind for each of the visions the words are painting. The three months of continuous rain that Moscow has been experiencing were arranged, I assured her, so she and the audience would have no trouble understanding the speech. Titania also has the right to a genuine anger with Oberon at the end of the speech. As we were working Masha, with studied casualness, informed me she had won a prize over the summer as best actress in a Soviet film festival. I congratulated her but I must confess I was a little surprised—she doesn't seem to be a particularly good actor. The prize was clearly of significance to her. Maybe it will boost her self-confidence in her work on Titania. While she has learned the lines beautifully, she ultimately does not have the power either vocally or internally at the moment. She is very snobbish about her ability to understand English and the fact that she doesn't need an interpreter when I talk to her (only when she has to talk to me). She's getting on

Helen's nerves. Working with the actors individually in the evening is a great pleasure. But what am I going to do about the set, the clichéd forest and the boring court? Have I simply bitten off more than the Pushkin can chew? They have not been able to make the vehicle for the mechanicals work. While they have the chassis of the invalid car (the motorized sardine can), they have no way to make it actually drive on and off. The technicians hooked up an electrical motor and were actually suggesting that it drive on with a cable dragging behind it. Then after installing it they decided that a cable with high voltage running through it was, in fact, too dangerous. It is not a huge demand to have a vehicle that actually works on stage. Except in Russia.

Yesterday as I was driving past the front of the theatre there was a huge, newly hung square banner covering the whole front of the building, announcing the opening of *Dream*. It had a Canadian flag in one corner and "Directed by Guy Sprung (Canada)" down at the bottom. Oh, my God! This isn't just a dream, it is real!

Wednesday, October 10, 1990

Theseus: Awake the pert and nimble spirit of mirth,
  Turn melancholy forth to funerals:
  The pale companion is not for our pomp. (Act I, scene i)

Sergei and three of the female fairies worked with Tanya on the choreography for "Over hill, over dale," the song we have turned into a vocal trio at the top of Act Two. Puck gets sexually teased and manipulated in what is an attempt to place very erotic connotations on the words. Unfortunately the voices have been taped along with the music. The Russians insist it is impossible to dance and sing at the same time. So I can either have them dancing and the voices taped or they can sing into a mike and hardly move. It is clearly impossible to try to teach them in a few weeks a century of musical theatre tradition. Nor are radio mikes an option. Mmm...

The sound technician was attempting to set up the area voice mikes (PZMs) I had brought from home. I explained for the second time how they work, but the crew steadfastly refuse to instal them properly. Is this some kind of Soviet one-upmanship? They still haven't found a transformer to get the DX7 working as promised.

The opening of the play will be very strong. We placed the Amazons downstage, blindfolded. They enter as if to be executed. Theseus stops the execution and goes down on his knee to beg Hippolyta to marry him. She agrees only after he has freed all the prisoners. I moved lines 16–19 of the scene beginning with "Hippolyta, I woo'd thee with my sword / And won thy love doing thee injuries" to the top of the play. This makes the situation crystal clear. When Theseus takes the blindfold off Hippolyta and they lock eyes, there is an instantaneous sexual tension between them, a result of the mental and physical respect they have gained for one another on the battlefield. They now have four days before the new moon when they will marry. "O, methinks how slow / This old moon wanes! She lingers my desires." In other words, four days of sexual tension before they will sleep together. It is this tension between these two opposites which provides the fuel in the engine of the play.

Then Tanya had the actors run Act Two. The movement of the students as they carry Sasha around the stage on his movable bower (a kind of wooden stretcher, really) is breath-taking. Has Sasha had something to do with the quality of the movement? I could see him in the background quietly manipulating the actors. The students carry the bower on their shoulders while Sasha stands erect on top. They raise and lower him like an elevator. He sits, lies, leans on it; it is home to him, a part of his anatomy. Masha has not got her female fairies under such control. They refuse to carry her, arguing she is too heavy. So Masha pouts. Tanya's three-year-old boy was in rehearsal, not for the first time because he was running around shouting, "*Otdei ribyonka*" ("Give me the boy"), one of Oberon's lines in his fight with Titania. Tanya's mother, who usually takes care of the child, is ill and Tanya can't afford to hire a baby-sitter. I will have to explain that Tanya must find some other arrangement. It is not fair to the actors or to me.

Helen told me I have the reputation of being very tough. People think I am a maniac, determined to get what I want. I thought I was being a push-over. Well, if this is my reputation, then it will probably make getting what I want a little easier.

We finally got to the finale. Arkady played the tape for the cast and starting tomorrow everyone will learn it. Tanya bitched about not getting the students often enough. At the moment they are still taking some classes so we have them four hours a day, maximum. Tanya and Sergei have an energy and drive to get things perfect that is similar to mine. This is good.

I had supper with Sasha, who talked endlessly about how much he loved Quebec City last June during La Quinzaine Internationale du Théâtre.

But here in Moscow the Pushkin is floundering financially. No shows are doing well and none selling out. Attendance is dropping, in part because people are simply afraid to go out at night. Funtikov (Bottom), Sasha said, is a very popular TV actor and has played in many children's films. He explained that Sergei is behaving well because he took him aside and read him the riot act. He told Sergei that if he didn't stop drinking then and there he would have him fired and he would never work in any theatre ever again. Sasha then went to the other actors and told them to confirm all this should Sergei ask. Outside of rehearsals Sasha treats Sergei exactly the way that Oberon treats Puck. Sasha also explained that before *Dream* Yury would not give him any leading roles. Now Yury is changing his tune and has offered him the lead in another play in the repertoire, replacing Oleg Antonov, the original Bottom. Sasha apparently told Yury that if he was forced to play the part he would leave the theatre. Like everything else in the Soviet Union the Pushkin has its hierarchy. You are either "in" or "out."

Another session trying to get Valery Barinov to inhabit a classical style. At one point, Elena (Hippolyta), who was with us for this rehearsal, jumped across the stage and did all of Hermia's lines, then jumped to another place on the stage and did all of Helena's lines. Impressive. She is still smarting from being offered what she sees as a part too small for her talents. Giving the royal couple some dignity and warmth in their interruption of the Pyramus and Thisby play in Act Five is difficult. It is an easy trap to let all the interjections be callous put-downs of the tradesmen as actors, so we tried to rescue some grace for the pair. Inevitably Valery and Elena asked about the long and puzzling discussion of the "hounds of Hercules" in Act Four. I explained that in Shakespeare a "dog" or "hound" often has the connotation of the male sexual organ (the opposite of "pussy"). In "their heads are hung / With ears that sweep away the morning dew" we can hear the sexual *frisson* between the two characters. Hippolyta's lines, "The skies, the fountains, every region near / Seem all one mutual cry," suggest, of course, a mutual sexual climax. The whole dialogue here is just dripping with poetic circumlocution of the sexual act. Theseus and Hippolyta are simply having a very difficult time staying out of the sack until they are officially married. Valery and Elena looked at me as though they can't believe Shakespeare really has so much sex in his plays. It is all there in the text, I keep telling them.

Igor, the driver, is getting a kick out of chauffeuring his North American tourist around. He loves showing off his prowess, slaloming around the pot-holes, overtaking two or three lanes at a time and, when we get stuck in a traffic jam, driving up on the sidewalk to avoid it. There are accidents everywhere. In fact I think we have escaped being killed about four times. Keeps you awake.

Thursday, October 11, 1990

Oberon: Fare thee well, nymph. Ere he do leave this grove,
  Thou shalt fly him, and he shall seek thy love. (Act II, scene i)

During the April rehearsals we were on the road to specificity with the roles of the lovers. Over the course of the summer a certain generalization has set in. Today's session was devoted to trying to re-hone the clarity of the four young characters. With each entrance and scene in the forest the lovers become more extreme versions of themselves until by the end of Act Three, scene two, when Demetrius and Lysander go into the woods to fight and Hermia chases Helena around the stage, they are nightmare reflections of themselves. Demetrius becomes a jock air-head, emotionally and verbally abusing Helena. Lysander becomes the wimp, manipulated and controlled by the rich bitch Hermia. Maria Andreeva has found a few nice comic moments to illustrate this. When Lysander tries to sleep beside her she puts her hands on her hips, stamps her feet and snaps, "*Lacg dalshe*" ("Lie further"). We've just seen Lysander enter the forest weighted down with a huge sack full of Hermia's wardrobe, while she runs on gaily chasing a butterfly with a butterfly net. Poor Lysander is learning the hard way the old maxim: "He who marries money will earn it."

We had settled the accents and the instruments for the mechanicals in April. (They were supposed to have been practising the live music all summer.) Snug is a Ukrainian fireman and plays an accordion; Quince is a Jewish carpenter and plays a *gellikon*, a Russian tuba; Wall is a Georgian bricklayer and plays the violin; Starveling is from the Volga and plays the bass drum; Flute is from Estonia and plays an old-style Russian wooden flute; and Bottom is a Muscovite Jack-of-all-trades who plays the balalaika.

"And I hope here is a play fitted." Some stage-hands pushed the vehicle for the mechanicals on and it certainly looks great—white graffiti and stickers on a blue body, even "ECS Group of Companies" scrawled on one of the doors by some enterprising props painter. Unfortunately the technicians still can't get it to work. They have promised that by tomorrow they will have the electrical cable hooked up so we can try it. The entrance of the mechanicals singing and playing as they ride on the vehicle will be a fabulous change of pace in the flow of the production. The new Bottom came to work, as I suggested, in a cowboy hat and boots and started strutting around the stage quite nicely. I also tried to trim some of the excesses of the actor playing Wall so he won't be noticed. With this group the key is to get them all to keep the scenes as simple as possible so they don't get in the way of the play.

Oleg Antonov, the original Bottom, dropped by at the end of rehearsal. We went off to eat together. It was like two dogs circling each other and sniffing. He said his production of *The Cherry Orchard* will be going to Toronto for six weeks in the spring. I couldn't imagine where they would be playing, but I didn't question it. He handed me a copy of a play he's written, translated into English by a theatre in Seattle as part of an American/Soviet reading exchange. (The protagonist has fled to his dacha where he spends the entire play trying to build a book shelf with the help of the local handyman. The piece is a nostalgic yearning for some undefined individualism, and totally devoid of any drama. You might call it a *perestroika* period piece.) His agenda was to be sure I wasn't angry with him for deserting the show and to fish around to see if I might put him up if he came to Canada. He also enjoyed taking a few shots. When I asked him if he thought *Dream* would get an audience, he answered with a grin, "Well, the first night anyway."

I explained I could understand his need to leave the production, but I was pissed off with him for not communicating with me and leaving me no time to deal with the situation. He just nodded. It occurred to me then that perhaps he had already known in April he would leave the production. I asked him if he knew any actors who might be good for the part. He didn't.

I sauntered through the lobby as the audience for the evening's performance of Dostoevsky's *The Devils* was gathering. The three floors of lobbies are relatively imposing, with the bright new murals and an extensive collection of pictures and archival material from the glory days of the

Kammerni on exhibition. The photos from Tairov's productions in the '20s, *Romeo and Juliet* for example, are extraordinary. The set is multilevelled, cubist in bold colours, and the costumes are equally unrealistic and visually stunning. One gets a feel of the powerful creative energy the theatre housed at one time. There is one very striking picture of Aliisa Koonin as Phèdre. I looked for a long time at each of the photos of Tairov himself, trying to understand what he might think of our production. It was a tiny audience dotting the lobbies, politely reserved, all older people. What on earth will *they* make of our production?

The evening was once again an attempt to hone the work of the lovers. Lysander's awakening is a complete and instantaneous flip into love for Helena. "And run through fire I will for thy sweet sake!" He hops around the stage like a pogo stick out of control. Over the body of the sleeping Hermia he spits hatred and then runs off. Hermia's erotic nightmare about the snake slithering up her body makes her awaken with a blood-curdling scream. Hermia then beats up on Demetrius exactly the way Demetrius had on Helena. Hermia finishes with a kick to his groin and exits. Demetrius falls to his knees in agony. "There is no following her in this fierce vein," he moans, and crawls pathetically along the ground and falls asleep. The actors are attentive and they are striving to explore their roles with intelligence and imagination. Working with them is a pleasure. At the end of the session we agreed on the short-term goals for each of them. Alexander must believe in the reality of Demetrius more. He is pushing too far in the direction of caricature. Maria must do the opposite and find ways of pointing Hermia's mannerisms more in the direction of comedy. Irina must find ways of keeping Helena alive and fresh and avoid falling back on juvenile-lead routine acting, and Andrey (Lysander) must speed up his delivery without ending up all on one note.

At the end of the day Helen and I went for a beer in the Intourist Hotel at the foot of Gorky Street. In theory only foreigners are allowed in. A group of shady-looking men at the door check passports. Helen, with her western clothes and sophisticated air, takes great pleasure in speaking loudly in English while staring at the doormen with total disdain as she pushes her way past. Nobody dares to ask for her papers. Everything in this country hinges on one's invisible status. In the bar, a group of American students were singing "One Hundred Bottles of Beer on the Wall" and generally behaving as if they already owned the place.

Early in the afternoon I had an argument with Valera about the poster.

He generously agreed to do the design himself after the initial design by another artist proved disastrous. He pulled me into Yury's office and the three of us looked at a clever, tasteful drawing of a butterfly with the head of William Shakespeare. I wondered how to tell this man whom I love and respect very much that I think this is a major mistake.

Finally I just blurted out: "A butterfly is way the fuck too light for our show. What the fuck is it doing on the poster?" I threw out some suggestions for improving it, like adding some eyes to the pattern on the wings or genitals to the body of the insect. The image could be of an ass with Shakespeare's head, Shakespeare could have ass's ears or be winking.

Valera resisted the ideas, shaking his head and muttering softly, "Guy, these are such difficult times. We need to look at happy images."

"Fine. Happy images, but let's at least have them have something to do with the play," I barked. Yury nodded. Valera frowned.[2]

Friday, October 12, 1990

Puck: *Up and down, up and down,*
     I will lead them up and down. (Act III, scene ii)

I've just come back from the Canadian Club at the Embassy and I've had a few too many Labatt's Blues.

Today was horrendous. I've said before I would throw in the towel, but now I mean it. I arrived early to watch the technicians set up the scenery. As the final ritual before every rehearsal, one of the young female stage-hands sweeps the entire expanse of the stage with a tiny, ill-made hand-broom. It is little better than the proverbial army punishment of cleaning the parade square with a toothbrush. Then they pushed the mechanicals' vehicle on stage, but eight technicians standing around couldn't figure out how to make it work. A simple technological problem but no one could solve it. The sound technician was attaching the PZM vocal mikes I had brought to the metal structure of the set. This means they will be very effective in picking up the sound of every footfall on the ramps but not too useful for the voices. When I explained yet again how the mikes worked, the technician took umbrage. "We know what we are doing. We are professionals," he said.

[2] A version of the final poster design appears on the cover of this book.

The DX7 is still not operational. They tried it with a Soviet transformer but it fried some of the circuits inside the synthesizer. Christ, it had better not be permanently damaged. Then I gave the mechanicals shit for not having learned how to play their instruments over the summer, and Funtikov forgot to go to wardrobe to pick up his cowboy hat and boots for rehearsal. In addition, I felt compelled to go over each scene with the mechanicals line by line because they were improvising too much and destroying the text. After that I was looking for things to throw. Then the lovers arrived but not the composer who was to work with them, and on his first entrance, Andrey (Lysander) slid on a nail that had been left on the stage and cut his knee, bleeding all over his costume. He ran off to soak it in salt water. The girls are also wearing finished bits and pieces of their costumes which look astonishingly ugly. Ksenia is in Denmark for the opening of an exhibition of her paintings so I have no one to complain to about the costumes. Nor did all the students turn up for the fairies' rehearsal. What do I do? How can I possibly get this show together? To top it off, according to Helen, my interpreter, I insulted the mechanicals by calling them "female slaves" when I thought I was saying, "Hey, guys!" in Ukrainian. I wondered why they had all suddenly looked so peculiar.

I fled to the basement of the Canadian Embassy where on Friday evenings they open the bar and the Canucks who live and work in Moscow can rub shoulders and get a hit of home to last them through the week. As I was nursing my umpteenth beer, I thought the man next to me looked slightly familiar. He was an Air Safety Inspector sent from Ottawa to investigate an accident with an Aeroflot plane that had occurred in Gander. He was staying at a hotel near the airport. He told me he had been here only four nights and had already experienced four separate shooting incidents in his hotel. As he was leaving his hotel this morning, he met a bedraggled Irishman coming in the door. The Irishman was one of the managers of the duty-free store at the airport and, apparently, as he and three other workers were coming back to the hotel last night with the day's takings, their cab had been attacked, guns blazing, by another cab. The Irishman had jumped out of the car and escaped across a field, and spent the night on foot finding his way back to the hotel. Where his companions had ended up he didn't know. Come to Moscow and experience all the thrills of the Wild West! It turned out the safety inspector was the half-brother of Rick McNair, the former Artistic Director of Theatre Calgary and Manitoba Theatre Centre.

As we were talking, the Cultural Affairs Attaché gave me a letter from Rita, from home. It was an envelope bordered in dark ink, and looked like it contained a funeral announcement. "Oh, my God," I thought. "Trisanna has died."[3] But it was her telling me that she made a will leaving me all her worldly goods should the plane crash when she flies to Moscow later this month. And she quoted an obscure contemporary love poem (in Dutch!). Death and Love. Love and Death. Why does everything at the moment, even a beautiful love letter, reflect the theme of *A Midsummer Night's Dream?*

Saturday, October 13, 1990

Puck: Fairy King, attend and mark;
  I do hear the morning lark. (Act IV, scene i)

Had a coffee this morning with Stephen Handelman, the Moscow correspondent for the *Toronto Star.* He is an immediately likeable man. Hunkered down in his office, surrounded by the weapons of his trade, computer, FAX, telex, he looks as if he has dug in for a long battle. He's been here over three years and, surprisingly, he still has a fire in his eyes lit by an inner need to know. He just came back from an island in the Pacific north of Japan, further away from Moscow than Toronto, where the Soviets are permitting a carefully watched free market to develop. Naturally, he explained, this little experiment in capitalism is being undermined by those who have privileges to lose, particularly the Communist Party members.

He asked me suddenly, "Why did you come?"

"Curiosity!" I replied. "And because I think Canadians have skills that they should show around the world more often."

Stephen feels strongly that culture, even more than economics, will be the ultimate battleground of the war fought for the Russian soul. The Russians' major worry about letting in western capitalism is the loss of their culture. In the Pax Americana that will follow the end of the Cold War, every major culture in the world will be fighting to survive the American cultural invasion. He reminded me of the five-minute strike that performers in Moscow staged in all theatres a few months ago, organized by the

---

[3] Our daughter. According to Rita, the ink was not black but navy, in an innocuous Laura Ashley floral design.

new Minister of Culture, himself a former actor, to protest against cuts to
the arts. At one point as we were talking, I veered into incautious territory.
He silently pointed to the ceiling to remind me of the hidden microphones
that are bound to be in the office of a western newspaperman. I gulped
and wondered whether I might have got some of the people at the Pushkin
in trouble.

"Don't worry," Stephen said, "they are usually off these days."[4]

I took my leave as he returned to his mammoth task of trying to keep
on top of the extraordinary metamorphosis of this vast *Zagadka*.

The weekend's usual children's matinées once again left me with few
actors to work with, this time only the students, Masha and Sasha. Tanya
gets very upset every time I suggest we can improve on the choreography.
She sees any attempt at change as a negative reflection on her work. This is
worse than silly. The *pas de deux* has a nice "dirty dancing" eroticism,
which we are improving and developing. But Titania and Oberon break
from their downstage positions far too early. They must wait until Puck
comes in with his lines about the "morning lark"; the dawn is their motivation to flee the forest. Tanya agreed to reblock it only after major pouts.
Finally, two hours into rehearsal the DX7 was successfully hooked up. It is
not broken!

Masha pulled a number when asked to rehearse her awakening (Act
Four, scene one). "Where is Funtikov! Why is he not here? I won't work
unless he is here too." Bottom's only contribution to the scene is to lie on
the ground asleep. I shouted at her that he is not here and isn't coming
and would she please get on with it. She lifted her chin, stuck out her chest
and we carried on.

The entire theatre is gossiping about the ugly costumes coming out of
wardrobe. Ksenia is back in town but hasn't turned up. We finally tracked
her down at the *vernissage* of an exhibition of paintings. She seemed a tad
wary as I grabbed her arm and pulled her out of the crowd. "We have an
emergency on our hands. We need you to come in and sort out the
costumes." She promised to come in tomorrow.

Helen continues to intrigue me with her determination to disassociate
herself from anything Russian. "I refuse to stand in line. I won't stand in
line for anything, even if they are giving out gold." She has a magical way

---

[4] Assia's daughter Tamara Galko has a great story about the omnipresent listeners in
the life of westerners in Moscow. In the middle of a telephone conversation from her
apartment in the diplomatic compound, a heavily accented voice broke in: "Could you
please just wait a moment? I have to change the tape."

of getting us into the supposedly booked-up restaurants by treating the doormen with silken haughtiness.

Sunday, October 14, 1990

Oberon: Thou shalt know the man
  By the Athenian garments he hath on. (Act II, scene i)

Someone plugged in the DX7 without using the transformer. It must be truly fried now. I can't believe it. There is now no easy way to attain any quality in the music. The DX7 is an older synthesizer by western standards, and nowhere near as flexible or astonishing as the more recent samplers or emulators on the market, but it was more than adequate for our needs, allowing us with the push of a button to create the sound of any instrument known to mankind in addition to any effects and electronic sounds we invent ourselves. Surely they haven't destroyed the whole thing? A replacement is too much money and too many miles away.

Ksenia was due to come to rehearsals for a mini-costume parade. But when the cast turned up there was no one from wardrobe to supervise the fittings. Ksenia, of course, was late. Over an hour behind schedule, the students started to appear wearing bits and pieces of the costumes. Nobody is as self-righteous as a student actor whose costume isn't looking right. I learned a new Russian word: *kashmar*. Like so many Russian words that pertain to theatre it is French in origin—*cauchemar* ("nightmare"). In Russian the word has clear overtones of "disaster." None of the costumes was near completion, many were too tight and, along with the ill-fitting wigs, they got in the way of all the elaborate movement Tanya had developed. The rehearsal hall was filled with a gaggle of bitching, swearing actors. Worst of the lot were Tanya and Sergei, running around and slagging off the designs. Ksenia arrived in the middle of this and, with a somewhat bewildered face, set about trying to regain both the look of the fairies as she had designed it and the confidence of the actors in what they will be wearing. Adding here, cutting there, she made a little headway.

I marched into Orlov's office and announced I thought we should cancel the production. "We can't pull this off," I stated bluntly.

I detailed the problems, he naturally agreed to help sort them all out. "What is the single thing that might expedite all this?" he asked, nodding his head in sympathy through a cloud of cigarette smoke.

"If we elevate Elena Shumskaya [the Stage Manager] over the heads of Marianna and Andrey, and give her the overall responsibility for all the organization of the production," was my reply.

As this week progressed, I became more and more aware of Elena's quiet force on the stage. She seemed aware of the problems but lacked the authority to deal with them. Earlier in the day I quietly sounded her out about the idea of taking over. She was eager and agreed it was the only solution.

Orlov over the last week began to lose some of his extraordinary *sang-froid*. It is easy to perceive: his face goes one degree darker red and he leans forward an additional quarter of an inch. This was what happened as he nodded that this shift in responsibility could be arranged. Of course by then I was back on board, and we agreed to initiate the new order by calling a full-fledged production meeting and arranging the schedule. We go into technical rehearsals in one week and I haven't a clue as to what has been organized.

Monday, October 15, 1990

Bottom: Enough; hold, or cut bow-strings. (Act I, scene ii)[5]

Elena and I sat down together and devised a production schedule we will present to the assembled heads of departments. She is happy with her increased powers, though worried that Andrey has not been officially told of the new arrangement.

"It is a moral problem," was her statement.

Yury, unfortunately, is somewhere in Siberia at a Theatre Union meeting (he is one of the high muckymucks in the newly constituted union). The problem is compounded by a deep-rooted sexism that will make the change tough on Andrey's sense of self-worth. I said I'd talk to Andrey first thing tomorrow.

[5] I've never found it so annotated in any modern edition of the play but I have always assumed that what Bottom is saying is "Hold fast" (as in defending a position against an attacking force) "or surrender" (the cutting of bow-strings being the traditional sign of a garrison surrendering). He is saying something akin to "Shit or get off the pot." At least that is how I mean it here.

Then Valera showed me the new design for the poster. He has Shake-speare winking and he's put ass's ears on his head; otherwise nothing is changed. Not the poster I would have chosen, but Marianna laughed out loud when she took a look at it, so it can't be all bad. In fact, everyone except me likes it.

Marianna and Elena were told twice, Arkady three times, that we are going to go through the music cue by cue, starting at one o'clock. We needed all the instruments on stage, the DX7, the drum machine and the violin with its electric pickup functional. At one o'clock the synthesizer is three floors up in the rehearsal hall, the drum machine is set up in the auditorium and the violin is forgotten about entirely. Someone goes to get the pickup. He comes back without the assembly instructions. Someone else goes to get the DX7. Then we test the drum machine and find it hasn't been set up properly. The DX7 is finally hooked up and, thank God, it actually works! But Arkady's script, still in loose pages, accidentally falls to the ground and the pages scatter all over the stage. Suddenly Arkady and one of the technicians are going around to each page and touching it with their bums. This is a Russian superstition. If pages fall to the ground you must sit on them before picking them up or you will lose your luck. One hour later than scheduled we got to the first music cue. I'm giggling now as I write all this down but I won't be giggling when we start tech rehearsals and have to add cues for lights, sound, the actors and the set, etc. Better not think about that right now.

Then Arkady started to play with his new western toy. Vikka, a skinny, intense and, I suspect, very talented piano player, wanted to sit down and learn how to master the synthesizer. (She'll be playing the performances.) Arkady wouldn't let her. He was having too much fun. We inched our way through the script, testing the appropriate buttons on the machine and stirring some darker shades into the music. Arkady doesn't seem to bother writing anything in his script. But Vikka, her head held high and covering her wounded pride with disdain for Arkady's disorganization, quietly made notes about all our choices behind his back. As we push for tougher, crunchier sounds the DX7, an old war-horse of a synthesizer, its keys battle-scarred with John Mills-Cockell's cigarette burns,[6] is enjoying the new challenges and seems to be guiding our search. Dragging it half-way around the world has been worthwhile.

[6] The Toronto composer who sold me the synthesizer.

A quick meeting with the literary manager, who in Russian theatre also handles the publicity. I try to push her to promote the show in a western manner. She responds with a list of the Russian and Canadian press she has contacted. The theatre is even buying taped ads in the Moscow subway system. She assures me there is a lot of interest in the show.

Then a quick solo rehearsal with Funtikov. He came prepared, with his cowboy boots and hat on, grinning and pointing to them as if to say, "Aren't I a good boy? I have remembered my props!" I have decided to go with him. He is bright, eager to please and a bit of a fool, a combination that might produce a creditable Bottom. We spent our time making sure he understands the text, and we decided to change the name of the character from "Assnova," meaning "foundation," to "Asslov," meaning "arse." Elena found me an actor who would be a more exciting Flute. Should I cast him and risk the ramifications? I'll sleep on it.

Igor had noticed there was temporarily no line-up at McDonald's and, wanting to bring me a gift, nipped in and bought a Big Mac and fries. He then walked in on our musical rehearsal and handed the stuff to me in front of everyone. When I tried to give him some money he waved me off angrily, "What do you think? I have no money?" With a car of his own to hire out, Igor is wealthy in comparison to the artists. Here I was being brought a luxury they could afford only if they sacrificed the basic necessities of life. They looked up, noted the bag and then looked away. I turned red with embarrassment and stuffed the bag behind the seats. Later I took the cold hamburger upstairs and gave it to Marianna. She wolfed it down with such violence that I couldn't watch. Christ, what a world! I wouldn't have the guts to try to survive here. My passport and my airplane ticket home weigh a ton in my pocket.

Later when Igor ate supper with me at the Dom Kino the invisible Soviet class system became apparent again. Igor, for all the hundreds of roubles in his pocket, was very uncomfortable surrounded by artists from the film world. He actually grabbed my coat as we walked in and was too timid to even order. The waitress immediately sensed he was a "nobody" and snubbed him. This quiet, self-contained young man, forever reading a novel while waiting for his always late, North American director to appear, is imprinted with some invisible status that can be read by every Soviet as clearly as a machine can read the electronic code on a credit card.

Afterwards we went for a walk on the Arbat, the picturesque, old part of town where artists and souvenir craftspeople line the walkway plying their wares. It felt as dangerous as walking down 42nd Street in New York. I kept my hand on my wallet and my head bobbing around nervously like a pigeon. Copious greasy adolescents offered to change money. In one store there were piles of loaves of bread for fifteen kopecs apiece and even coffee beans, a pound for the equivalent of a day's wages for an actor. But there was no meat at all and there was a long line of people at one counter selling lard. In a tiny antique store I found a perfect pince-nez for Quince. Now he will look more like Trotsky than ever.

Don Murray, the CBC Moscow correspondent, told me over the phone during the day that Gorbachev had won the Nobel Peace prize. When I passed this information around the theatre everyone was furious.

"What good will this do us?" hissed Valera through clenched teeth.

When I came home tonight I turned on the news to watch the press scrum around Gorbachev as he fielded questions about his laureate. He looked exhausted, vulnerable, slightly confused. The Russians hadn't placed their president behind any slick podium for the occasion. Is this a lack of marketing smarts or a deliberate attempt to make their leader look like one of the people? When asked what it felt like to be the first communist to receive the honour, he replied, "Well, it feels normal."

He was pleased. No poker face could have been able to hide that. An American correspondent asked him if he thought the honour would help his internal politics. Gorbachev gently denied it would have any impact.

Tuesday, October 16, 1990

Snout: O Bottom, thou art changed! (Act III, scene i)

With Orlov beside me I tackled Andrey first thing this morning. Trying to be politic, I explained that I needed to rehearse under conditions more familiar to me, where the assistant director worked with the actors and the stage manager organized the rehearsals. He sat silently, very hurt but, like a true Philostrate, made sure it didn't show. Orlov was no help, but his presence acted as an official stamp of approval.

Helen has some of her Belgian business connections visiting town for two days so I have a new interpreter. Nina is a single mom who shares a two-room apartment with her mother and her two daughters, and supports them all on sixty roubles a week. She speaks no English, only French

and German, so my brain is sizzling a little as we alternate among four
languages in rehearsals.

Stephen Handelman turned up to watch our work, grinning the whole
time. I think he thinks I'm crazy. We tried to clean up the first chase, the
mechanicals reacting to Bottom's ass's head, then being chased by the
fairies through the forest. There are lots of gymnastics from the students
and bodies being thrown around the stage.

Tanya whined the whole time. "What are we going to do? The car is in
the middle of the stage. How do we block around it?" I made what
seemed to me to be reasonable suggestions but she rejected them all.

The music is too long so I asked Arkady if we could cut some. "Nope,
can't be done. It is on the tape."

Tanya whines. Arkady is obstreperous. Through it all, Funtikov is
striding around like a parody of the Marlborough Man. What better way to
illustrate the one character who in the course of the show loses his identity
than by having him assume American traits and in doing so become an ass?
The props department devised a splendid ass's head with a functional lower
jaw, and Bottom's voice is clear from inside the mask. But Funtikov has
never really done any work with masks and can't invest the being with life.

At one point, I suggested to the mechanicals that Starveling should be
eating sausage during the scene. "There is no kolbasa to be had anywhere.
How can she eat it if there is none? *Eta nasha shizn.*" ("That is our life.")

Afterwards at the production meeting, there is a consensus (at least
that's what I was told) that Elena's new position is a good one. We
hammered out a production schedule. Lots of nodding heads. (This is too
easy, I thought.) Ksenia complained that the actors aren't showing up for
their costume fittings and that she is wasting her time. An argument
developed as to whose responsibility this was. She agreed she could be a
little better organized.

Wednesday, October 17, 1990

Oberon: This is thy negligence. Still thou mistak'st,
   Or else commit'st thy knaveries willfully. (Act III, scene ii)

We worked on the fairies' break-dance at the end of scene two in the third
act. It is long and confusing and boring. Some simple trimming will give it

life. Tanya continues to pout. She and Sergei now lead a voluntary warm-up session for the actors every morning. So she stands there afterwards, slightly sweaty, her hands on her hips, staring at me with anger in her dark eyes. Sergei stands half a step behind her in support. He is aware that she is acting up a little but he supports her anyway. It is driving me insane. Finally we started haggling as though we were in some Oriental bazaar. If I accepted one of her suggestions she would accept three of mine. At least the ending of the scene is powerful. Oberon climbs the back ramp, watches the goings-on in the forest, and then by raising his hands freezes the action and rolls all twenty or so bodies on stage with one movement upstage and off.[7]

Of course it again took two hours for the technicians to figure out how to hook up the DX7. And again the PZM mikes were hooked up incorrectly. By the end of the day Nina, the new interpreter, was sagging from trying to keep up. Though the finale was clearly printed on the rehearsal schedule the musical director didn't show up to work with the cast.

My dreams are amazingly vivid here. As we get closer to opening they are becoming more concerned with the production. Last night I dreamed I was sitting at the back of the auditorium with the entire cast. In total silence, the entire fly-gallery, the sets and the curtains started to collapse in slow motion onto the stage. As it all settled with a great cloud of dust, the actors turned around in unison and looked at me. I suggested we go out into the street and perform under the trees of the boulevard in front of the theatre without sets or lights or music. They all agreed.

Thursday, October 18, 1990

Oberon: ... lead these testy rivals so astray
As one come not within another's way. (Act III, scene ii)

While Tanya was working on choreography with the students, I was initiated into a Russian-style press conference. In Orlov's office, with journalists from *Tass*, *Isvestia*, *Moscow News* and *Soviet Life*, I attempted to explain what we are doing with the production. My outline of the images of "hot

---

[7] During the previews and the opening the audiences responded to this business with enthusiastic and spontaneous applause. According to Elena, they still do.

ice" and "merry tragedy," as well as the concept of the show, fell on very deaf ears. The questions when they came were very basic.

"Do you enjoy working with Soviet actors? What do you think of Russia?"

I expressed my honest admiration for many of the artists I am working with, though I left room in my answers for interpretation. A steely-eyed woman from *Tass* tried to pin me down on whether or not I thought the Pushkin was a good theatre. Circumlocutions abounded. Inevitably they raised the question of what it is like to work in a foreign language. This opened up a subject that threatened to actually be about something. I tried to talk about language as a handle on the suitcase of reality, explaining that just because we had a hold on the handle didn't mean we knew what was in the suitcase. We use this handle (language) to drag many preconceptions around with us, and working in a foreign language can give us a chance to examine these preconceptions. I explained that I was less frustrated working on the play in Russian than I was trying to understand the world I am working in. In retrospect the press conference was a disappointing anticlimax.

The literary manager has not been around the rehearsals at all during this month. Am I paranoid or is she always off in a corner whispering to someone about the production? She seemed to corner a few of the journalists when the session ended.

We slowly worked through Acts Four and Five. Having decided it is too late to make any more cast changes, I tried to get very specific with the mechanicals and their comic business. We worked for a while on the play-within-the-play. Quince's *gellikon* is large for him and it has provided the root for much silliness. After playing a piece of music immediately upon their entrance, the "rude mechanicals" bow to the court, who is sitting in the first rows of the audience. Quince bows so deeply, with his tuba still coiled around his head, that he cannot bend back upright. He starts to keel over toward the front of the stage. The weight of the instrument keeps him waddling forward, to the increasing consternation of his fellow thespians. Just at the point when it looks as if Quince is going to fall off the edge of the stage into Hippolyta's and Theseus's laps, Starveling rushes forward, grabs him and helps him stand upright again. As she is still carrying a huge bass drum strapped to her front, she inadvertently hits Quince and knocks his glasses off his head. Now he is really stuck because he can't see without them and he can't risk bending down again to pick them up. He whispers for help into the mouthpiece of the tuba. Starveling finally locates where her name is coming from and whispers back by sticking her head into the opening of the tuba. When she eventually realizes the problem and bends down to pick up his glasses she, of course, with the drum strapped on, rolls forward as she tries to grab the elusive glasses, etc. etc. Comic business that must be timed and played with total conviction or it will be an irritating waste of time, rather than a charming exploration of the life of these characters. We made some progress, though I'm still begging my Theseus for a more "classical" delivery.

Just when I thought the day was over it truly began. Ksenia and Masha had a blazing row during a costume fitting. While Masha was wearing her partially made costume Ksenia took a large pair of scissors and started to cut away the fabric. Masha resented being treated like some tailor's dummy and declared she would not wear the costume, apparently feeling it made her look fat.

"Find another actor!" she screamed.

Ksenia screamed back that they would do exactly that. Soviet actors have the right to refuse to wear their costumes. At this point Ksenia came running to find me and Masha went home. While a great designer, Ksenia is not a theatre person; she just doesn't understand how difficult it is psychologically to get up in front of an audience and act. If Masha doesn't feel sexy in what she is wearing on stage, she won't be able to be sexy in her scenes. Ksenia declared all this was nonsense and stated categorically that if I begged Masha to wear the costume then *she* would walk out. The whole business was ludicrous. There we were, more than half a dozen grown-ups, myself, Ksenia, the interpreter, Marianna, Elena, the seamstress and some curious bystanders, crammed into the narrow hall outside the fitting room, and all screaming at one another. I promised to talk to Masha in the morning. Elena suggested that since Masha trusts the seamstress the best tactic might be to work with the seamstress to refine the costume in a way which would allow Masha to feel proud of her look.

A week ago I accepted an invitation to Sasha's place for tonight. It was a relief to flee the theatre and head over there. Yanina has just arrived from Toronto to take on the interpreting duties again so with two North Americans in his apartment Sasha was doubly anxious. His wife must have been cooking for a week. From his balcony he showed us a great view of the skyline of Moscow, including the red star on the Kremlin in the distance. Below, across the road from his apartment block, are a park and a small pond.

"There used to be a lot of ducks in the park. Lately people have been catching them to eat," he said. Thus began an evening of Sasha's venting his anger with his own country.

"Russia is one of the richest countries in the world. We have gold, we have oil, we have wheat. Why can't we live properly?"

Supper was a roast goose. "Is this from the park across the road?" I asked.

"No," he replied, "it is a Hungarian goose. I found it at the market by sheer luck. The potatoes and raspberries are from our dacha."

They both watched our every mouthful solicitously. Later we caught the latest news on television from Sasha's native Ukraine. The student pro-democracy strike in Kiev is at its peak. Sasha admitted he has long since thrown his party card away. He is skeptical that any true change is going to happen. He loudly berated all Soviet playwrights for not writing anything relevant to what is going on in the streets. He sees major changes coming in the theatre and has yet to decide what he will do about them. He too might leave the Pushkin and become independent. Then he quizzed me about our production. He seemed to be asking whether I am trying to produce an apology for the current political system. His questions hinged around the wording in Oberon's final speech. In our version this is a singing finale with the full cast accompanying the Fairy King as he blesses the marriages. Shakespeare's lines, "So shall all the couples three / Ever true in loving be," are translated into Russian as: "Let happy and successful be their union in everything." The contentious word is "union" which of course in Russian is *soiuz*, i.e., the Soviet Union. The translation is from the '30s. Is there a hidden pro-Soviet message in the lines? Am I missing something here? I promised I would find the right opportunity to clarify the meaning with the whole cast.

This evening for the first time I understood the attraction of the Russian way of drinking tea. Black, with a little raspberry jam stirred in. When it is home-made raspberry jam, the tea has a tangy sweet schizophrenia that is unique and very beguiling.

Saturday, October 20, 1990

Bottom: Take pains, be perfit; (Act I, scene ii)

I missed last night's session with the diary because I came home drunk on Polish vodka after a dinner with Ksenia and Elena that was intended to calm down the troops, but which I obviously exploited to try to calm myself down.

We had our first full run-through yesterday. Naturally we waited for half an hour before we got started while the sound technician resoldered the power cord to the DX7. Meanwhile I gathered everyone together and tried to outline the game plan.

"Fore-check in the corners, and take the puck away from them. Check check check!"

Nina, who was spelling Yanina off today, looked at me as though I had lost my marbles. I insisted she translate literally. My attempt at humour drew blank stares all around. Again I casually mentioned that the name "Puck" means *schaiboo* or "hockey puck" in English. Sergei Agapitov looked at me quizzically.

The first half is one hour and fifty-five minutes, the second is nearly one hour and thirty minutes. This is a disaster. The whole play can be performed in English with no intermission in just over two hours. The acting is turgid, self-conscious, precious, introverted. The actors are also inaudible. On the plus side there is a complex layer of mirrored images and echoes, subtlety side by side with brashness, that is true magic at moments. In the middle of addressing the assembled cast after the run, I inexplicably became vehemently angry and began to berate them loudly.

"You're a bunch of rank amateurs, lazy and incompetent, and you don't deserve the name of actors."

I singled out Egeus for behaving as if he was in a kids' matinée and Demetrius for forgetting every bit of blocking and business we had rehearsed. From now on, I told them, I expected them to think, work, live and breathe the production. Where does this nascent tyrannical behaviour in me keep coming from? Agapitov had a look of panic on his face as I spoke. Tactically, blowing my cool could only weaken myself in their eyes. They shuffled out, ready to start a week of technical rehearsals on Monday.

A quick parade of the costumes that are ready followed. The mechanicals' costumes are disappointing. With the exception of the fireman's costume for Snug, none has the oversized clown look I had asked for. None of the shoes is oversized either. The head of wardrobe just shrugged her shoulders and said they don't have big shoes. They took the costumes away to try to give them a larger look. The Amazons aren't willing to wear their costumes as Ksenia has designed them, with one nipple protruding though a slit. But Theseus has a wonderful white uniform, very suggestive of Stalin. Masha managed to escape without having to put her costume on, so now I have to wait till Monday to try to solve the "big problem."

Today we did some work on the music with Sasha and the student fairies. Sergei, who was called, didn't come. He phoned in to say that he had twisted his ankle during yesterday's run and that he needed to take the day off. Tanya and Sergei continue to work the fairies like fiends, driving them into the ground as they try to achieve perfection in the movement.

Sunday, October 21, 1990

Puck: *And this weak and idle theme,*
  No more yielding but a dream. (Act V, scene i)

Another strange dream. I was watching a gymnast who was a little overweight and somewhat clumsy (in other words, me) perform in a big room of a rather glorious house. High up on the mantelpiece of a three-storey-high fireplace was another gymnast, the catcher. The heavy-set gymnast performed a complicated tumbling sequence which ended in a high back flip. For a moment it looked as though the gymnast on the mantelpiece was going to be able to catch the first gymnast on his shoulders, but then the two bodies fell slowly forward into the abyss. Just as another me, perched on some ledge half-way down, was leaning forward to catch the two men I awoke to the sound of the telephone ringing. It was Rita, calling from Toronto to tell me in a sombre voice about Trisanna's tumble from her little friend's stroller and that she had to take her to Emergency at Sick Kids. She seemed a little worried about actually coming to Moscow after this incident.

On Friday I pulled Tanya and Sergei aside and asked them not to be so negative about rehearsals and especially not about the costumes in front of the actors and Ksenia. Today we re-bonded our working relationship and sat down and talked through the whole production, analysing every piece of choreography and determining what could still be trimmed and what needed clarification. Tanya and Sergei have not had the resources to feed their child properly for weeks. Yet they are militantly proud. When a parcel from Assia arrived for them Sergei apparently had a fit.

"Why do I need to accept gifts? We are not beggars!"

When we carried on our deliberations over a working lunch where the meal cost their entire month's wages, they immediately turned to ice. With an extraordinary self-discipline, they made sure that at the end of the meal there was still plenty left on the plates. Their eyes kept flicking back to the food but they wouldn't give in.

I was reminded of a statement a Russian had made on a previous visit: "If there is war between America and Russia we will win because we know how to do without." I wrapped the food up in a doggy bag and ate it myself later. Once again Sergei didn't show up for rehearsal. Today he didn't even bother to phone to cancel.

Monday, October 22, 1990

Quince: ... to bring the moonlight into a chamber; (Act III, scene i)

A long and hair-raising day, the first day of tech week in the theatre. One tiny legacy of my work at the Pushkin is the introduction of the production table. I insisted Elena be in the house with me and I asked the carpenters to build her a large table over two rows of seats as the centre of her operations. When she was seated there behind a microphone and linked to all points in the theatre I felt calmer. We were to have a sound-cue rehearsal while the stage technicians finished rigging the set, but the musicians didn't appear and the mikes weren't set up. The great production schedule was shot even before we started. After much grumbling Valera agreed to bring in the iron fire curtain to start the show. It makes a stunning first image as it slowly rises to reveal the court in place. Everyone is concerned it will get stuck on its way out, as it has done in the past, and then they will have to perform with it half-way out for the whole show or else cancel the performance.

A proper lighting rehearsal didn't happen either. The set was late getting up and then the "master of light," as the lighting designer is called here, was late setting any light cues. But I was intrigued by this dried

walnut of a man. Without paperwork, without having done any home-
work, he walked from instrument to instrument, getting the crew to focus
around the stage and insert gels. How did he know what he was doing?
Some major Zen lighting experience was happening here. When we finally
got to setting a few cues for the court, I was quite stunned. He knows
what he is doing, but I sure can't see how he is doing it. When the official
rehearsal time ended, he came over. "I know in the west you have unions,
but here we don't," he said. With that he just carried on working.

After yet again explaining to the sound crew how the PZM mikes work,
I went off to the much-awaited costume fitting with Masha. Three seam-
stresses, the wardrobe mistress, Ksenia, Masha, Elena and myself crowded
into a tiny fitting-room. Masha has the foundation to her costume on, an
imitation leather swimsuit, and she is so foul-tempered she won't look at
anybody. I ask for the sketch to remind ourselves of what we had agreed
the costume would look like. It can't be found. Someone describes how
the boots are to look and how the gloves will fit. The tension between
designer and actor is unbearable so I rudely ask Ksenia to leave the room.
Masha lets a thin smile flit over her lips. The wardrobe mistress then
becomes very active and starts to drape and trim material over Masha. We
work out how the flowers can come out of the boots to make Titania look
as if she is growing out of the ground. This is the image Ksenia had
designed. It is special. The bathing suit definitely emphasizes Masha's hips
but the wardrobe mistress manages to turn what Masha herself regards as a
defect into an extraordinarily seductive asset. Masha actually begins to look
a little happy about the result. The problem now is the lack of time to
finish the costume. At Elena's insistence, leaving Masha behind but picking
up Ksenia en route, we all stomp off to Orlov's office and deliver an
ultimatum: the costume must be finished overnight. Orlov nods. He and
Ksenia wander off to the wardrobe department to discuss how this can be
achieved. I become hysterical.

"Don't let Ksenia back in the same room with Masha!" I flee to the
production desk, my sanctuary. Fifteen minutes later Ksenia returns.

"It is all over. We are back at the beginning, Masha won't wear the
costume."

I blow up at Ksenia, "Why did you go back in that room?"

She turns on me, "Why did you kick me out?"

"Because I am trying to get your goddamn costume on the goddamn
actress!" I snarl. I have no idea where we go from here.

Tuesday, October 23, 1990

Pyramus: Thou wall, O wall, O sweet and lovely wall, (Act V, scene i)

I am now screaming at everyone. Perhaps I should take out Russian citizenship papers. Must be careful, though, for while shouting is often the only way to get things done, I may end up pushing people too far. It is going to be a hard week, and I don't want to drive the cast and the production into the ground.

Perhaps I will lose my mind first. Sergei still hasn't turned up, and can't be found anywhere. He lives a totally vagabond existence and no one seems to know where he is staying. The consensus is that he is on a drunk with some of his circus friends. The theatre is sending a car tomorrow to an address they have for him outside Moscow. They will tie him down and bring him in so I can talk to him. Marianna has that "I told you so" look. Well, she did tell me so, but an alcoholic Puck is still better than any Puck the Pushkin could have given me.

Masha. Wardrobe bought a pair of boots for four hundred roubles, but Masha claimed they were too big and clumsy. They had to be scrapped. She will realize at some point that she is cutting her own throat, won't she? After all, she is planning to actually go out on stage, isn't she?

We managed to work through the whole of the first half. By trimming lines from the lovers and trimming the choreography and speeding everybody up, we have cut, I would judge, about twenty minutes. We roughed in lighting cues and sound cues. But since each operator takes his cues on his own recognizance, rather than getting cued by the stage manager, I found the process utterly confusing. How do they ever get the same timing and the same feel twice in a row?

The opening is sensational. The audience walks in and sees a heavy metal wall in front of them. The house lights snap to black and the wall slowly begins to rise, as the imitation Soviet anthem plays. From behind, the light shines through the widening crack as the wall inches up to reveal the imposing court set and the soldiers preparing for a firing squad. It is a stunning opening by any standards. Valera, however, insisted again that it is too risky to use the fire curtain because he is sure it will break down. The electric winches that operate the curtain continually burn out. Altogether, Valera is driving me nuts. He continues to insist we change the uniforms so they don't look so much like Red Army uniforms.

"They should come from the world of the play, not our world," he keeps whining.

The mechanicals' vehicle broke down and no one can figure out how to make it work again. So I have thrown in the towel on ever getting a motorized entrance and, justifying it to myself as a Brechtian in-joke, I will let two stage-hands push the vehicle on in full view of the audience.

Tanya explained that the front half of the Pushkin is built on the site of the house where Rasputin first stayed when he came to Moscow, and the back half of the theatre is built on a cemetery. More dark associations. The fun has left the show for me. Why am I here? What am I trying to do? The fights with Valera have taken the joy out of the work.

Don Murray and a CBC crew arrived at the theatre to tape some rehearsal. The cast cheered when they learned that in return for permission to do this the CBC has agreed to contribute a couple of cases of Canadian beer to the opening night party. Realizing they might end up on western TV, all the younger women in the cast ran to the dressing-rooms to put on make-up. Don was pretty morose about the whole thing. I guess covering culture has little kudos. No doubt he prefers modelling his leather jacket, with the Kremlin as a backdrop, while striving to give weight to his history-making news reports, forcing his voice to sound as deep as it can.

At the end of the day, as the exhausted actors were leaving to catch the Metro home, word came back from the dressing-rooms that someone had stolen all the students' watches and wallets while they were on stage.

Wednesday, October 24, 1990

Hermia: I am amaz'd, and know not what to say. (Act III, scene ii)

We continued the work-through, timing the scene changes in the second half with the lights and sound and the actors' entrances. Keeping the lights in the forest dim and mysterious, while focussing enough on the faces of the main actors, was difficult. The "master of light" solved this by having two technicians full time on two instruments which continually move to pick up Oberon and Titania. These instruments are not follow spots so their movement is very jerky and obvious. The operators have to anticipate the movement of the actors. Like everything else this technique means relying on the memory of the operators. Will anything ever be done twice the same way? The "master" speaks some German, so we can almost communicate. At times I wonder if this is what it might have felt like to direct in East Berlin. Inexorably we move forward, hampered in the after-noon session by the fact that we still have no Puck, and all the actors are tense, wondering how *this* problem is going to be solved. As I am about to go off to supper with Valery Barinow and Elena Skorokhodova, Elena Shumskaya pulls me aside.

"Masha is having a fitting," she says. "Come."

They haven't found a smaller pair of boots and Masha is still complain-ing that the large boots are too slippery. I suggest an insole, she shakes her head. One of the cutters suggests some rubber soles on the bottom; Masha hems and haws. I shout at her that she is being a silly twit. She gives me her best innocent, hurt look. Why is she being such a cow? Her costume could steal the show! I stomp off in a rage.

Supper with the two actors was a slightly stilted, formal affair. Valery, as befits his seniority, is a member of the theatre's artistic council and insists on behaving with a very old-fashioned dignity. He treated Elena Skorokhodova with a mock chivalry appropriate to a Czarist officer. He carefully agreed to only a tiny glass of vodka with his meal, because we still have work to do. I was happy to play along with the atmosphere he set and, with great gentility, the three of us touched upon the obvious topics of conversation. How did he enjoy Canada? (He had been to Quebec City with the Pushkin's production of *Ward Six.*) "Very beautiful city," he maintained graciously.

We talked about the difficult times in Moscow, and Elena of her dream of living in Paris. On the walls of the Maly Theatre Club Restaurant, where we were eating, were photographs of many famous actors from the Maly Theatre. He was able to identify each one and also tell a little story or anecdote about them. My agenda was simple. I needed these two actors to be more supportive of the production and I needed a Theseus who spoke up and could be understood. At the appropriate time, I gave them both a few notes to that effect. The three of us solemnly agreed to work together over the next few difficult days.

Back at the theatre I was told Masha had declared herself ill and gone home. I climbed the stairs to Yury's office and asked him to intervene. Yury had yet to appear at any rehearsals but I was pretty sure he was getting daily briefings about the problems of the show. He didn't bat an eye when I stated my request and reached her on the phone straight away. His tone was suddenly soft and reverential.

"How are you, Masha, my dear? Is it serious? I am so sorry to hear this. Masha, we have a terrible time problem and we would appreciate if you could come back to the theatre. Just sit in the auditorium and read your part. That would help so much. Thank you, Masha, my dear. You are so wonderful."

She agreed she would come back tomorrow. Goddamn Russian actors! Serves me right for shouting at her.

Then I was told Sergei had been found. The theatre posse had located him and, as requested, brought him back. In Orlov's office, with Elena and Marianna and Orlov himself, we confronted him. Marianna immediately started to scream at him. "Where have you been? Why didn't you phone? What kind of irresponsible action is this?"

His eyes bloodshot, his hair standing scruffily on end, he looked at us with an impish grin. "I tripped during the run-through and sprained my leg," he said.

Then he unwound a bandage and revealed an ankle that didn't look swollen, but was covered with some horrible-looking brown liquid. (Painted up?)

"I couldn't walk," he wailed, reeking of alcohol.

Marianna seemed determined to engage him in a shouting match. I couldn't be sure she wasn't trying to get me to fire him. I shut her up and decided to take Sasha's tack first off.

"You'll never work again in any theatre in this city, if this gets out. You'll be finished as an actor."

He shrank marginally, trying to put up a little resistance, but eventually admitted that what he had done had been irresponsible. I cleared the room.

"Are you prepared to commit yourself to coming to every rehearsal from now on and never repeating what you have done?"

"Yes, of course!" he replied.

"Look me in the eye and say that," I demanded.

"Yes, of course," he repeated. His eyes were soft, frightened, desperate.

"I have taken a great risk in casting you in this part and I deserve an honest answer."

"I promise I will be there."

I believed him. I told him that I wondered if, after the run on Friday, he had panicked when he realized for the first time how big and important his part was and how much work he still had to do on it.

He looked at me and said with great relief in his voice, "You're right!"

We shook hands and he wobbled down the stairs, less because of his ankle than the booze, I suspect. I'll have to touch base with him once a day, just to reassure him.

We ploughed on through the second half, Sergei getting all his entrances and his exits wrong, forgetting his lines, and treating Sasha and the rest of the actors with haughty hilarious insolence. Something very Puckish was coming out of this drunken midget, and I would have been laughing except that the entire cast was furious that he was being allowed to behave this way. Sasha, of course, was steaming, as was Andrey Dubovsky. They just shook their heads in disbelief and anger. Half-way through the evening, after I had shouted at Sergei yet again for being in the wrong place on stage, he wobbled over to me in his dishevelled red tracksuit, put his hands on his hips and looked up at me with defiance in his bloodshot eyes.

"You know, ever since you told me that 'Puck' also meant '*schaiboo*,' I have understood the part," he declared.

At the end of rehearsal, the actors inexplicably clapped.

Saturday, October 27, 1990

Pyramus: O grim-look'd night! O night with hue so black!
  O night, which ever art when day is not!
  O night, O night, alack, alack, alack, (Act V, scene i)

It is Saturday morning and I've got two days of diary to catch up on. As the rehearsals get more intense, it is more and more difficult to find the energy each night. In addition, Rita arrived on Thursday and that shifted the focus of things a wee bit. She has gone off with Helen to Zagorsk for the day. I am looking out my window on ten huge, colourless apartment blocks, each one with at least a hundred apartments in view. At night when I come home, I like to look out at my thousand television screens and wonder what scenes of Soviet soap opera are being played out. Today is a grey morning, even the clouds look as if they have a layer of dirt on them. In the three weeks since I arrived, the leaves on the birch and linden trees along the streets below have fallen. Across the way, every balcony has laundry out to dry. A couple of wizened old ladies are bending over tubs and wringing their washing out. From below, the sound of children playing in a hidden park wafts through the window.

Sergei Tsvetkov told me yesterday that in one of his dreams he and I were caught in a huge tank of water, desperately trying to escape before we drowned. Last night, I dreamed I was in the auditorium watching a television monitor of myself on stage rehearsing. I was in slow motion, whereas the entire cast was being fast-forwarded: I just couldn't think fast enough to keep up with everyone.

Thursday morning we worked with the technical crew, determining the precise moments when the half-dozen hanging gauzes that are the moveable forest get flown in and out to support the action of the play. We want the forest to be alive, to react to the events occurring in it. The forest comes down and surrounds the lovers as they are getting deeper into the woods. During the break-dance or the chases, the forest "dances" with the fairies. When Oberon gets angry the forest flies rapidly out, afraid of the wrath of the King of the Fairies. All this is possible only because the size of the crew is limitless, by Canadian standards, and one fly-man can be assigned to each line-set.

Tanya tried to do some more work with the students, but half of them are sick with exhaustion and malnutrition. I managed to continue some precision rehearsal with the clowns. Quince's précis of the play-within-the-play, the dumb-show, is now hilarious. He gets more and more involved with his own words as he describes the story, finally working himself up to the point where he grabs Pyramus's sword and "kills" Thisby himself. We have established one very chilling moment. After Theseus interrupts Bottom's lines with "The wall, methinks, being sensible, should curse again," Bottom, his tiny fake sword in hand, walks towards the Duke to explain that he was merely giving Thisby's cue. Suddenly all the lights in the theatre snap on and the soldiers move forward with their rifles, pointing at the mechanicals. Petrified, they throw their hands up, Bottom dropping his sword. Theseus, knowing there was never any threat to his person, waves the soldiers off, the lights dim again and the play continues. For a brief second, Soviet Russia was on the stage.

Because of the cast changes, the mechanicals' music is still very rudimentary. Snout's violin is non-existent, Flute is still frustrated by his flute and Snug has not really mastered his accordion. All those months wasted! I was hauled into the foyer to check on Masha wearing the beginnings of her redesigned costume. She is still petulant. We agreed to add more foliage to disguise the size of her hips. The costume can't be finished for a week.

Valera and I had another set-to about the soldiers' costumes. Is the mirrored reality on the stage too blatant? Is the Stalinist uniform and moustache for Theseus excessive? Will the audience react with hostility? I will have to watch the previews carefully and see if I have made a mistake.

I spent much of Thursday looking at my watch and saying to myself, "Rita is in London now" or "Rita is at Moscow Airport now."

The tech dress Thursday evening was predictable. We are now using many of the costumes. When the anthem played and the curtain rose, only one Amazon of seven appeared on stage. She started giggling, then all the other actors joined in.

"Where the hell are the rest of the Amazons?" yelled Elena.

Half are ill and at home, the other half hadn't been given enough time to get their costumes on. We started again. Sergei was still shaky on his blocking and only carried his skateboard around. In the first forest scene, when Masha caught a glimpse of Sasha in his costume, she burst out laughing. Sasha's costume has a very strong sexuality to it. It includes a studded piece of leather that hangs between his bare thighs. He struts around, obviously loving it.

"The costume is a gift," he confided later.

But for Masha, seeing him thus the first time was too much and she cracked up.

"What the fuck do you think you are doing?" I shouted at her from the house. (Remember, she understands English.)

As the run continued, I noticed I have developed the late John Hirsch's habit of snapping my fingers loudly if a scene is too slow. We came to a full stop again when the first scene with the mechanicals arrived and there were no stage-hands to push the vehicle on. This was a ploy of Marianna's to try to get me to have the actors push it on themselves and save on stage-hands. I refused to let the actors do it and was promised that tomorrow there would be two men standing by for the entrance.

The worst element of the show is still the singing. The two moving lights are always late following the actors and hence very distracting. But Pyramus's death is hilarious. I patted Puck on the head at the end of the day.

Friday morning was devoted to all the problem scenes in preparation for a second dress run in the evening. The weakest moment by far is still Act Two, scene one, the first scene in the forest in which three of Titania's fairies dance Tanya's intricate choreography while lip-syncing to the tape of professional singers. The whole thing is a masterpiece of bad planning on my part, and artistically a total mess. I can't see any simple way to clean it up. Because he is such a strong, clear presence and can afford to lose a few lines, I cut all of Puck's subsequent long speech ("Thou speakest aright..."), trying to get to the entrance of Oberon and Titania as quickly as possible. But I can't cut the whole introduction to the forest, or we have no build-up to the battle of the Fairy King and Queen.

The intermission is set at the beginning of the long lovers' quarrel (Act Three, scene two), immediately after Hermia's entrance. Puck has followed Hermia on stage, smelling something in the heavy bag she is shlepping. In a moment of irritation, he freezes the action of the lovers and, with the four statue-like figures silent on the stage, he opens the bag to discover a McDonald's take-out Big Mac and fries. He smells the chemical fast food and grimaces, throwing the hamburger away in disgust and kicking the bag. With a reluctant shrug, he pulls a traditional Russian pretzel from his own pocket, snaps his fingers, and two fairies in waiters' garb bounce out, placing a glass of tea on his skateboard in front of him. Making it clear through his demeanour that he is eating this meagre fare not out of choice but out of necessity, he sits down and has his intermission snack. Almost as an afterthought, he signals to the technicians to bring the house lights up and the curtain in. Nice bit of business that will give a little edge to the rest of the play. When the curtain goes up at the end of the intermission, Puck has finished his snack. He wipes his mouth with a serviette, burps and then, winding the lovers back like a tape in fast reverse, he re-starts the action. The rather long scene then becomes, as Tanya and Sergei have devised it, a boxing, wrestling, kung fu match in a roped-off ring the fairies have set up—a great kick-start back into the second half. We added the mechanicals to the lovers' chase at the end of this scene. Driven in a panic by the invisible fairies, they run on from all directions and meet in the middle of the stage. There is a brief moment of respite, as they rediscover one another and assume they are safe. Then the fairies grab each of them and throw them toward the edge of the stage. The house lights flash on, the clowns see their worst nightmare (the audience), panic even more and run back off the stage. At the end of the run-through, we tried to invest the finale with some vocal life from the cast. Little luck there.

Not everyone made it to rehearsal. Valery (Theseus) has a high fever and will be out for a few days, and Elena (Hippolyta) has food poisoning. One week to opening. If the large brush strokes are in the right place, then many of the smaller details should fall together of their own accord, as we run it more often.

Sasha and I walked shoulder to shoulder through the Friday evening crowds along the boulevard to have dinner at the Maly. I feel quite close to this eager, talented Ukrainian. The commitment and the speed with which he got behind our outlandish production were some of the main reasons I was able to carry on. Despite my broken Russian, we managed to cover the bases of male conversation, from politics to women and children.

The evening run was exhausted and empty, but from the structure of the hollow shell it was possible to glean considerable hope for the coming week. The first half is down to an hour and a half, and Act Two is an hour and ten minutes. We have cut forty minutes in one week! Not bad. (Orlov was very relieved. "People want to go home, Guy. The streets are dangerous.") A few funny moments when Andrey, the Assistant Director, who was reading in for Theseus, also had to play two scenes with himself as Philostrate. The lovers are really speeding up their scenes and, in so doing, have honed their characterizations nicely.

The students playing the Amazons sewed up the slits in their jackets. They don't yet convey a strong sense of militant feminism, with or without the exposed breast, but feel like a group of student actors on stage. For some reason, the seamstress took all the foliage from the waist of Masha's costume and sewed it around her arms. This means her waistline is more exposed than ever, and she is unhappier than ever (with reason). Again I patted Sergei on the head and praised him. I'm trying to keep the father-son relationship going, to help him through the next week. He is happy; he knows he is doing a good job. He won't bolt again. I called the actors into the auditorium and thanked them, finding some nice things to say about many of their performances.

Sunday, October 28, 1990

Prologue: If we offend, it is with our good will. (Act V, scene i)

Yesterday, with Arkady, Vikka and the violinist, but without the actors, we reviewed every piece of live music. Now that we are all more familiar with the possibilities of the synthesizer, we analysed every choice we made and found greater variety and subtlety. Sergei Tsvetkov was with us as well. He acted all the parts and did all the blocking; he even gave many of the lines to help us with the timing. He was a marvel.

With Helen translating, Rita and I visited the home of Alexandr Gelman, one of the senior playwrights in the Soviet Union today. While doing a brief stint as the interim Artistic Director at the Vancouver Playhouse, I programmed the English première of his Shavian comedy of ideas, *We the Undersigned*, a pre-*perestroika* play examining many of the faults of the Soviet system. The production was a great artistic success in British Columbia and the translation we commissioned recently played to great acclaim in London and Glasgow. Alexandr is now a deputy in the huge Soviet People's Congress, and had a large hand in writing the recent freedom of the press legislation.

"Now that we have freedom of the press, all other freedoms will follow," he declared with a smile.

He has not written anything for the stage in the last five years (as Yury had said), and will readily admit that this is because, right now, real life is too important and too confusing to determine how to write about it. Five years ago, when we first met, he was a very unhealthy-looking, chain-smoking writer. Since then, he has given up cigarettes (one of the few Russians I've met who has) and now exudes an air of ebullient good health. A number of his plays has been produced recently in the west and, thanks to this modest good fortune (in hard currency), he was able to provide a very nice bottle of French red wine. I choked on my first sip as he softly informed me, in reply to my question, that he had never received a cent in royalties from the Vancouver Playhouse. It was humiliating to think that some cheap general manager had decided, because Canada doesn't have a copyright arrangement with the Soviet Union, to save a little money by not paying a Russian playwright!

We talked about the growing anti-Semitism in Russia. As a prominent Jew, Alexandr is spearheading the battle against it. He seemed compelled in his own living-room to play down the enormity of the problem to his western guests.

"In extreme times, extremism comes to the fore. But the numbers are not that large. Look at the elections in Moscow and Leningrad, the vast majority of the people voted for the democratic parties."

The passion with which he grabbed hold of the subject belied his attempts to defuse the questions. He also talked about the future of Soviet theatre, and explained that the government is drafting unemployment insurance legislation which will allow managements to fire actors. He confirmed what Yury had told me in April.

"Already many artists are being hired on a contract basis, which means they are not guaranteed permanent employment." He was determined, with his quixotic smile, to be philosophic and positive about the future.

"People are not starving," he stated, shaking his head.

I wondered what Tanya and Sergei would say to that assertion. Alexandr, in my view, is one of the world's great living playwrights. He has an ability, unlike any other playwright I know, to capture the quintessence of a political dilemma through the confrontation of very real characters. I have a very great admiration for his craft. I asked him about Tairov.

"Stanislavsky, Meyerhold and Tairov, the three greats!" he burst out, waving his arms. He explained that Stanislavsky was the theoretician, Meyerhold was the dictator and Tairov a mixture of the two. Tairov could achieve the same outrageous performances and striking effects as the mad artistic dictator, but he did it by getting the actors excited and understanding what they were doing. Meyerhold's method, on the other hand, was to simply order them to do it.

"What Russian theatre needs now is great actors who are true stars and who will attract audiences back into the theatres," he said. "We will soon see the theatre showing the dark side of what is being hidden from the public at the moment."

I asked him to come see our production because I need an outside eye to tell me if some of the associations and the characterizations are inappropriate.

I finally felt ready for another visit to Tairov. I've been having little conversations with him in my mind since my first attempt to reach him in April—and especially since June 4th. In the meantime I had read his *Zapiski reshiziera* (*Notes of a Director*). It was clear we had very different ideas about what theatre should be. I am much more of a populist, while he believes in a select, informed, initiated audience. But I am creating and working in a different time and am from a different country; perhaps this accounts for much of the difference in our perceptions of what is right and wrong.

It was another wet, grey day. I stood in front of the black marble gravestone of Tairov and Koonin and let my mind search out into the "undiscovered country" to reach him. Theatre in Canada, until recently, has been a process often of reinventing the wheel. My generation has not had any mentors. I have never had anyone with whom I could talk who might have helped me understand the fundamentals of producing theatre. Our theatre history is woefully short, and our record of passing down experience and craft from one generation to the next is lamentable. I hoped he would understand I have had to learn often by getting my fingers burnt. Often making the same mistakes a few times before I finally did learn. Would he mind if I talked to him a little?

"Please forgive my growing giddiness, my excitement about the opening, but I feel that we are within striking distance of actually pulling the production off," I began. "You and I differ greatly on our theories of theatre, but I am genuinely in awe of the photographs and set designs I have seen of your shows. You have guts and vision and your productions have a fabulous brashness.

"Perhaps we do share something? Can you understand why I feel it necessary to have contemporary images on the stage? Why I think that *Dream* has some relevant observations on the changes occurring in Russia now? Would you forgive my North American ignorance in tampering with elements from your troubled country? I realize that walking around with a Canadian passport and ticket home in my pocket makes my understanding of Russia paper-thin, and that my motives are suspect and possibly trivial at times, but I wouldn't be here if I didn't think, deep down as an artist, that I have a very strong and valid reason for doing what I am doing, even if the reason is beyond the realm of logic. Please forgive me my need to be successful in conventional terms with this production."

I explained what had happened at my own theatre over the summer and knew he could understand what I had gone through. I wondered if he would mind if, in the future, I kept talking to him from time to time.

I looked up to find an elderly gentleman staring very oddly at me from further down the path. He scampered off when he saw I was all right.

Monday, October 29, 1990

Prologue: The actors are at hand; and, by their show,
  You shall know all, that you are like to know. (Act V, scene i)

It's midnight. I'm trying to understand and replay in my mind the first preview. We had an audience of four hundred, mainly senior actors from the theatre union, who were invited free of charge because, as pensioners, they have little money to spend on theatre tickets. A potentially conservative and daunting audience. They were very quiet during the first half; the ice-breaker was Puck's business with the McDonald's hamburger just before the intermission. From then on they were enthralled. They loved Puck, they adored Bottom, they applauded the break-dance. At the end they stood up. This is exactly what the actors need. It will give them a boost in morale and energy down the home stretch this week. The lights and sound are dangerously unspecific, but I am not alarmed because it is not a disaster. It merely destroys a crispness to the spectacle. I have to admit that the timing is improving and the "master of light" uses every available moment to hang another light or focus another lamp or change a gel. He is dogged. The play does take a while to get started.

Seven more nights before we fly home.

Tuesday, October 30, 1990

Theseus: We'll hold a feast in great solemnity. (Act V, scene i)

I've implemented a new procedure for giving notes to the cast. From a store taking hard currency, we got a mess of cheese and bread and salami and cookies and coffee, and strung all the tables in the actors' buffet together. We called the actors in for a brunch and they all turned up on time. As they ate, they listened intently while I went through the production in detail. The cast was all smiles. There was excitement, there were jokes. They finally have confidence in the show. The rounds of applause last night during the play-within-the-play caught them off guard. They never realized how funny it was. Their friends and fellow actors in the house came backstage after the show to offer congratulations. They now smell the whiff of success.

In great spirits, we then worked with the musical director on all the music in the play, including the finale. The technicians have finished the prop candles the cast turn on as we sing our imitation "Ode to Joy." We also reworked the curtain call. Tanya and Sergei insisted that, as a final gesture, the soldiers come forward and discard their rifles in a heap and shake hands. It is the right final touch.

A Parisian director from the Théâtre Lucernaire watched a little of the rehearsal and then we went off together for supper. He is living in the Lenincomsomol Theatre. They simply threw out the Communist Party reps installed there and turned the office into a studio apartment for visiting artists. He is directing a French musical for the theatre and we swapped Moscow horror stories, our experiences being roughly comparable. His show was programmed to open mid-December but he is certain this will translate into mid-February. He is determined to hold off the opening until the production is ready. He felt that being a westerner in Moscow at the moment must be similar to what it felt like to be an American in Paris after the war. With very little resources one can live like a millionaire. His Gallic energy was a welcome relief in sombre Sovietland.

Our first paying audience. Tickets are sent to three hundred kiosks around the city and one can never be sure until the last moment how many have actually been sold. Helen noted a "Sold Out" sign at the box office and saw people being turned away, but when the curtain went up the house was far from full. When commercial theatre is introduced, they will have to find a different box office system. Tonight I watched from the director's box. The show struck me as cold and slow. Theseus, however, is coming back to life after his recent illness. The mechanicals, who assumed they are the hit of the show, abruptly became slow, indulgent, messy and muddy. Everybody was upstaging everyone else. The actor playing Wall, in particular, started "acting" again, and if you are a terrible actor you had better stay away from acting. I wanted to wring his neck.

At the end of the performance, deputations came from the actors requesting permission to delay the start of rehearsals so they could sleep in a little tomorrow.

"Rubbish," I replied. "We have too much work to do."

"Easy for you to say," countered Marianna. "You have regular meals and get driven to work."

Ouch! But I didn't relent.

Six more nights before we fly home.

Thursday, November 1, 1990

Puck: Now it is the time of night
  That the graves, all gaping wide,
  Every one lets forth his sprite, (Act V, scene i)

Time is moving so rapidly and my mind is so numb it is hard to keep events in any kind of order or perspective. Wednesday morning the actors straggled into rehearsals exhausted and late. When we finally started working through from the top of Act One, Elena's, Tanya's and Sergei Tsvetkov's jaws dropped as I jumped in and out of the scenes, cleaning up the blocking, trimming lines and sharpening the focus.

"You mean this is not a run-through? We are going to change things again?"

Then they excitedly got into the act, and for four hours we pushed, pulled and dragged the actors through the first half. Much was "silk degrees," tiny adjustments intended to give the actors greater certainty and precision, to clarify moments and entrances. I was very hard on the mechanicals, in order to make sure they ceased their amateur upstaging. At times, I just wanted to nail their feet to the stage so they would stop moving around. With Funtikov, it was a question of getting him to rediscover some of the charm of Bottom's character. He was taking my suggestions about turning into a North American too far, grabbing his balls at every opportunity and generally becoming a disgusting idiot rather than a charming fool.[8] Funtikov is another alcoholic in the cast and his faculty for self-judgement has eroded. We trimmed lines from Hermia's scenes; the young actress's inexperience was taking her down the road of indulgence. Greater precision on the sound-cue levels, particularly the live violin, also helped.

Our third audience, on Wednesday night, applauded when Puck went through his routine with the McDonald's hamburger. The first half is now down to one hour and twenty-five minutes, the second half is sixty-five minutes. This includes audience reaction.

The mechanicals have come to me and asked me to change one of the lines. In Act Four, scene two, Flute says, "And the Duke had not given him sixpence a day for playing Pyramus, I'll be hanged." We had translated this

---

[8] A few days previous, I had taken away his cowboy hat in an attempt to rein him in a little.

into "six roubles a day." This is in fact the average salary in a State-run theatre. The actors were embarrassed by this and wanted to revert to the term "zloti," a Czarist coin. I asked them if the reality of their existence wouldn't help make a statement about the need for change. They didn't want reality. It humiliated them, was their reply. We changed the line. Bottom was particularly bad this performance. He mumbled all his text into the stage floor, and Oberon is responding to the growing self-confidence and audience appreciation of Puck by slowing down his own delivery, trying to get more stage time for himself. This is dragging the forest scenes.

This morning, we worked through the second half with the same precision and detail I insisted on yesterday. The actors are truly winding down, and wonder why we still have to rehearse as we are already performing successfully to audiences. Sasha surprised me by saying in the middle of rehearsal that he had to go home for a nap.

"You can nap all you like after the opening tomorrow," I barked, "but now you have to work."

Everyone is a touch testy. We did some very good work detailing the casting of the spells upon the lovers. In a ritualistic manner, with a slow half-twist of the hand, both Puck and Oberon squeeze the magic juice into the eyes of the intended victims. Lysander, Demetrius and Titania, in their respective scenes, bend forward in their sleep like zombies, arch their backs as if coupling with an imaginary partner, let out a groan of ecstasy and melt back into a prone position.

The mechanicals are still atrocious on their instruments. Vladimir in particular is complaining that his instrument doesn't work and he wants to hum his music. This would be embarrassing. Funtikov, Vladimir and I worked for a considerable time trying to get each of the deaths just right. Bottom's must be the comic death to end all comic deaths. He slits his wrists and cuts his heart out on the line "Die, die, die" and with every stab of his toy sword he pulls red ribbons (blood) from his sleeves and the inside of his jacket. (I have stolen the idea from one of the productions of the play in High Park in Toronto.) Funtikov is inconsistent, but in the past few days, he has held the audience with his comic talent so effectively that the audiences roar with laughter and time seems to stop. Vladimir as Thisby is a different matter. In a ridiculous wig and silly female garb, when she kneels over the dead Bottom and says, "Asleep, my love? What, dead, my dove?" the audience naturally continues to respond with mirth. In rehearsal today, I again tried to impress upon Vladimir the fact that by being totally serious, by being quiet, genuine and intense, he can take this comic mode, this comic state of being, and lift it into a different reality. Lines such as "His eyes were green as leeks" will, of course, encourage laughter if Thisby plays them one way, but it is possible for the same words to be used to invoke the all-consuming power of true love as well as the ridiculousness of infatuation. Played absolutely genuinely, the journey through Thisby's final monologue to the moment when she softly takes Bottom's sword from his armpit, where Bottom has lodged it, and brings it gently to her breast, will be through a secret passage from the realm of comedy to the realm of tragedy. The depth, power and scope of true love can suddenly overwhelm the stage. Vladimir doesn't believe this is possible to achieve. He wants to continue the laughs and top Bottom's death with the silliness of his own. Again and again, I tried to explain that something special is there for him to accomplish. This would be true "hot ice," this would be a true epiphany of comedy and tragedy co-existing in the same moment. Sergei watched me giving these notes to Vladimir, and his eyes popped as he realized what I am after.

"This would be amazing if we could do it. But this takes a master!" he said.

Yes, it would, I think, and Vladimir is not that. Where is the original actor I cast for the role and why isn't he here?

We cut more of Puck's lines. Tonight he entered through a trap below the stage and out of the base of one of the pillars for his "Now the hungry lion roars" monologue, bathed in strong green lighting from below. Nice moment.

Masha is still very upset about her costume. I asked Yury to talk to her and I also tried to make her feel better, as she sat in silence in her dressing-room, tears rolling down her face. Thanks to some further miscommunication, Wardrobe has put the foliage back around her waist and this, combined with some cutting Ksenia did around the shoulders and neck of her "bathing suit," resulted in her looking a little like a sumo wrestler this evening. Poor Masha. I've really screwed this one up.

The audience still takes a puzzlingly long time to warm up to the production, though both yesterday and today most of them stood up for the curtain call. Vladimir followed my instructions to the best of his ability during Thisby's death. It half-worked. Afterwards, I rushed to him to try to make him understand that though he hadn't pulled it off, and though I

could see he is still skeptical, he must not stop trying. I begged and
pleaded. He nodded half-heartedly. Puck is flying. He has many moments
when he has the audience totally mesmerized, or roaring with laughter. He
does a great imitation of a rock star, belting out his spell on Lysander and
manipulating his microphone like Mick Jagger. We open tomorrow, or
rather later today.

Four more nights until we fly home.

Friday, November 2, 1990

*Bottom: The eye of man hath not heard, the ear of man hath not seen, man's
hand is not able to taste, his tongue to conceive, nor his heart to report,
what my dream was. (Act IV, scene i)*

I've just come from toasting brotherhood with a large-bellied stage-hand,
one of the technicians who pushes the vehicle on for the mechanicals. I
ended up drinking in the crew room after the cast party broke up, and
noticed his Montreal Canadiens T-shirt. He gave me a big hug when I told
him Montreal was my team. Laughing, he struck Ken Dryden's famous
pose, one arm dangling over a pretend goalie stick.

"Ken Dryden, Guy Lafleur," he boomed.

Suddenly we were brothers and drank eternal friendship and unity
between Canada and Russia—again and again and again.

The day had started with a final brunch note session. I gave a few small
suggestions to the actors, something for each of them to work on to take
their minds off opening-night jitters. Once again, I attempted to outline
what the production is after. I reminded them that Shakespeare doesn't
have any messages or solutions. He only has a genius for understanding
human nature and the human condition, and his plays have to do with
people and places and real experience. I'm not sure I was in any condition
to make sense. I thanked them for the patience they have had with me, for
their generosity in letting me work with them, and for their courage in
rising to the challenge. At the last moment, I decided I wanted to take up
Valera's suggestion and added some multicoloured ties to the soldiers'
uniforms to distance them just a shade from the real thing. I also asked
Valera not to wear his Stalin moustache. The play needs to be more
sympathetic to the audience right from the beginning. Valera was right all

along. He listened in silence when I let him know what I was doing. At the end of the note session, Tanya came over grinning. She and Sergei had been sitting at opposite ends of the table. They had both been absent-mindedly folding a small piece of tin foil from a cigarette package. At the end of the session, they accidentally showed each other what they had folded. Identical little swords!

I had hoped to find time to get to the *Toronto Star* office to phone Assia, but time had collapsed and I never got away. Just before the curtain, an interview with Soviet TV proved to be another farce. It took them twenty minutes just to decide where to place one interviewer, one inter-viewee and the interpreter.

The house was nicely full. The play started slow to my mind. I fled before the end of scene one and climbed the stairs to the toilet next to Orlov's office. Yes, it was nerves, not a normal occurrence for me back home. As I sat there, perched precariously on the broken plastic toilet seat, a seat that was broken when I first met it, so to speak, two years ago, and had not been fixed since, I heard coming through the wall behind me the dim voices of the actors and the play. The wall of the toilet was the wall of the auditorium. So I sat there, my bare ass hanging out, and listened to much of the rest of the first half in solitude. A novel way to "see" one's own opening night. Knowing when a laugh line might be coming up, I would strain to hear the audience's reaction. There, disappointingly quiet from where I sat, was the laughter from the house. It seemed far, far away.

I was overwhelmed with a director's post-partum depression. My job is finished, I'm unemployed, I thought. I was depressed by my own work. The production was dead, unfunny, horrendous. It had not achieved all I wanted. I had disappointed myself. Maybe there was another profession I would be good at. In my mind, I went over my association with the Pushkin and tried to pin-point all the mistakes I made. All the while, the show was lumbering forward behind me, the tiny voices of the actors barely reaching me. Finally, I buckled up my courage and went back down into the house.

The audience still seemed slow and far away. Masha's costume was still not finished and I felt like a real asshole for coercing her to carry on regardless.[9] I was pleased with some of the visuals of the set and the forest, and we had made the palace look acceptable, thanks to some careful

[9] As late as December 20, 1990, Masha's costume still wasn't properly finished. See Appendix C.

lighting. Vladimir came on humming without his instrument and later insisted his flute had got "lost" sometime before the show. A disgusting actor's trick, to "lose" a prop one doesn't want to work with. Most of the Russian actors weren't flying. They had not taken the work we had done, incorporated it into their souls and then raised the level of their performance by a kind of artistic alchemy. I sent a message backstage for Bottom to be louder and faster for the second half. By Pyramus's death, the audience was loving Funtikov. Puck, Oberon, both rose to the occasion, and when Sergei ran forward for his final monologue, "If we shadows have offended...," there was a look small of panic in his eyes. Was he thinking, "If I can just get through this last bit then I will have done it"?[10]

As is the European custom, Tanya and Sergei pushed me out on stage towards the end of the curtain call. By this time, most of the audience was on its feet and clapping rhythmically. With moist eyes, Sergei presented me with a balalaika and sheet music for Bottom's song, signed by the cast. I looked out into the house and had to admit that it felt good.

Orlov had bought champagne and I had given Igor forty dollars Canadian during the show for vodka.

"No problem," he said. "The cab drivers have everything."

During the second half he found me in the theatre and whispered, "I got fifteen bottles." The Canadian Embassy and the CBC contributed cases of Canadian beer as well. So it was a good party—many emotional leave-takings and thank-yous. Andrey, the Assistant Director, told me he thought I had successfully yoked together east and west. (I don't think so.) Andrey Dubovsky and Maria Andreeva thanked me for not being a Russian despot and said my gentler methods had succeeded in releasing more creative energy in them as actors. Sasha declared I had helped him discover the "romantic" in him. At one point, I think, I climbed on a table and proposed a toast to Tairov, the Pushkin and to crazy Canucks. Yury came over and thanked me very formally for giving his theatre such a wonderful production. "You have given us a real gift."

On my way out, I passed the crew room and saw a very drunk Bottom surrounded by all the techies. They grabbed me and pulled me into the smoke-clogged room, asking fiercely, "So, what do you think of Russians?" It was then I was rescued by the Montreal Canadiens T-shirt.

[10] In her December letter Elena also stated that the mainly young audiences consider Puck to be the "pearl" of the show. See Appendix C.

In truth, I don't know what to think of the show. Three more nights before we fly home, but I won't get to see it or the actors again because it is not in the repertoire until next Tuesday.

Saturday, November 3, 1990

Pyramus: You shall see, it will fall pat as I told you. (Act V, scene i)

Rita and I spent the day drinking more good French wine at the Gelmans'. We all jokingly agreed to shoot a film noir set in present-day Moscow, with our Puck in costume being chased in taxis because he had somehow got hold of the Czar's crown jewels. We also jokingly agreed to start a Canada-Russia joint venture importing packages of cigarettes with a condom attached as a marketing device. (Both cigarettes and condoms are in short supply.) Alexandr ruffled my hair avuncularly, saying he had enjoyed the show, although he wasn't totally convinced about the need to Russify the mechanicals.

Then souvenir-hunting with Helen on the Arbat. Helen, who sleeps with lights on for fear of burglars, and who, with her hard currency made from translating, has been able to renovate her apartment so nicely that her neighbours called the militia in to check on her, this week acquired a very expensive fur coat which she can't wear anywhere because she would be mugged. We stopped by the theatre to pick up a rare book from the archives to look through pictures of past productions. On Marianna's desk was the stage manager's report about the afternoon's children's matinée. The entire stage crew had still been drunk from the night before and many of the scene changes were fouled up. While we were in Marianna's office, Yury came upon us inadvertently. The first look on his face seemed to say, "You again, I thought you'd left." But he quickly switched to an energetic reiteration of his gratitude.

Lots of phone calls from friends, and friends of friends, who were at the show and were overwhelmed. Reviews in Russia take up to six months to appear, but then the production should last at least five years in repertoire if the Pushkin survives.[11]

[11] See Appendix D.

Monday, November 5, 1990

Puck: I go, I go, look how I go,
  Swifter than arrow from the Tartar's bow. (Act III, scene ii)

Once again, and for the last time on this project, I'm in the departure lounge at the airport waiting to board. Yesterday was the usual crazed dash to stuff as much as possible into the last hours. First Izmailova and more souvenirs and then some delicious chili and eggs in Stephen Handelman's westernized apartment. He told a lovely story about visiting the KGB Museum which has just been opened to the western press (but not yet to the Soviets). While examining organograms of the Socialist Revolutionary Party of the early '20s, he came across a relative of his, a Misha Gandelman, in a party cell in Leningrad. He had also just covered the first gathering of former Russian nobility since 1917. Organized by someone claiming to be a descendant of Nicholas II, it included Soviets from ex-Stalinist generals, with their medals on their chests, to waiters from Paris. Apparently, many had the distinctive Romanov physiognomy. The *Toronto Star* is fortunate to have this quality journalist as their Russian correspondent.

Then a farewell supper at Elena's, the kind of boozy, sentimental evening that makes one never want to leave Russia. At one point, I took off my jacket because the crowded room was too warm. Later in the evening, Tanya asked me to stand up, close my eyes and hold out my arms. She put my jacket back on me and I opened my eyes to see that she had sewn the epaulettes and buttons of a Russian general's uniform onto the jacket. Everyone gave a mock salute.

"Now you're a true Russian general," they smiled.

It was an exhibition of a kind of human warmth that is so staggering it made me feel lead-footed in my waspishness and at a loss as how to return it.

We had promised Valera we would end up at his studio. By now we were running a few hours late. When we finally arrived, this generous, brilliant artist was waiting in the street for us, totally plastered. A happy drunk, I thought. We traded hats as we wobbled arm in arm down the street to his studio.

"Now I am Guy Sprung, and you are Valery Fomin," he said, tapping my hat on his head and collapsing into a paroxysm of laughter.

We entered the studio where his wife, Natasha, was waiting. She too had obviously been tippling. Once again, looking around the very nicely set up, large, single room that is his studio and looking at the extraordinary imagination of the man as evidenced by his drawings, I was very impressed. The identity swap continued to be the major source of entertainment.

"Come, give me your passport. I am Guy Sprung now. I am going back to Canada tomorrow and you will live here for a year. What do you think?" Suddenly it was no longer a joke. Exhausted by his life in Russia, he was needling me about my life of ease in Canada. I wondered whether, if he knew what my mortgage payments were and that I had no idea how I was going to meet them in the next few months, he would be quite so cavalier about the luxury of an artist's life in the west. But he was hitting home.

Natasha then started to attack me, at first politely, about the allusions in the production to Soviet life. "You don't understand Russia!" was her general drift. I ventured to suggest that perhaps they should not let foreigners in and then they wouldn't have to put up with our having any opinions or impressions. The conversation was drifting towards viciousness.

"You can't possibly understand what we've endured in this country," she snapped with genuine hatred.

"Russians don't have any monopoly on suffering and they certainly don't have any monopoly on understanding human nature," I replied with equal venom. "If the Pushkin Theatre wanted me to come here and produce a boring piece of antiquated theatre like the production of *Desire Under the Elms* currently in repertoire, then Yury should have told me that from the beginning."

Valera tried to calm me down, interjecting remarks like, "Women say a lot of nonsense. Don't listen to her."

This catapulted Rita into the fray: "I'm deeply offended by your stupid misogynist remarks." And so on. A painful way to say goodbye, painful because it contained considerable truth.

What will the production look like after it has played for a year? Natasha, in a side squabble to our main argument, insisted that, once I left, all the actors would breathe more in their roles and improve greatly.

Like some medieval wheel of life completing a cycle, the early morning drive to the airport was through a primordial deluge. The feeble, over-tasked wipers of Igor's Lada whined pitifully as they occasionally gave us the briefest of visions of the watery universe approaching. With unerring

instinct, Igor managed to find every submerged pot-hole. We were heading home—home, with its own share of problems, but where the questions
are easier. The economic state of the Soviet system, started with such
idealism, is like a battlefield littered with the carcasses of good intentions.
The desperate need for the population to experience immediate gratifying
changes in their style of living is creating such a tension in the country that
it is impossible to imagine how it will end, other than in a bloody *kashmar*.
If you believe in the possibility of socialism, or worse, if you believe in the
necessity of some form of socialism to ensure our survival on this earth,
then Soviet Russia right now will put those convictions to a terrible test. As
we sit here waiting for the flight to be called I feel exhausted and a
desperate need to get home to my daughters, my study and my old-timers'
hockey.

* * *

As we were on the point of leaving his studio, Valera gave me a small
drawing of a distorted bird's eye as a memento. The pupil is the focal point
of a spiral that disappears into infinity. I have it over my desk.

   In April, Assia had found a carved wooden ball, the size of a baseball,
bought for me from a craftsman from the Caucasus who travels to Moscow
to sell his wares on the Arbat. It has twelve holes in it, about the size of
quarters, and inside this ball is carved another ball and inside that another.... Seven wooden balls all carved miraculously one inside the other
from a single block of wood. An undertaking of skill and patience. It is, in
fact, a replica of a pre-Christian artefact of some kind, and represents the
seven spheres of the universe (very Elizabethan). It sits on my desk, too. I
won't claim to understand Russia any more now than when I first went to
Moscow, but in front of me as I work, I have two small emblems of the
great *Zagadka*.

Appendix A

[I wrote the following article about my first trip to Moscow for the Spring 1986 edition of the *Toronto Free Press* (Vol. 2, No. 3), a newspaper-cum-program I created when Artistic Director of the Toronto Free Theatre.]

European Diary: Part III, Moscow

by Guy Sprung

One of the first Western clichés to be challenged, even in a short, eight-day visit to Moscow, is the fallacy that Russian theatre is devoid of politically or socially critical content. As part of the official celebrations commemorating "Forty Years of Peace" (the end of World War II), Robert Stura's company, based in the province of Georgia, had been brought to Moscow for a limited engagement. Stura's company, known outside Russia as a result of an acclaimed appearance at the Edinburgh Fringe Festival, is obsessed with examining tyranny. Previously, they've adapted Shakespeare's *Richard III*, and their new work, *Judgement Day* (ostensibly about the Nuremburg Trials), draws parallels between Stalin and Hitler. Performed in Georgian, the play required simultaneous translation for the Russian-speaking Moscow audience.

This play blatantly compares past (and by inference, present-day) Russia to fascist Germany. Stalin is represented by a huge statue that dominates the stage, while Hitler is portrayed as a tiny man, desperately trying to live up to Stalin's image and stature. Shown Russian movies to inspire his own fascist propaganda, Hitler is depicted praising Stalin, emulating his actions. At the end of the play, Hitler warns ominously and melodramatically, "I may be back. Be careful, be careful ..." as he descends into Hell and the goose-stepping Russian soldiers march in to occupy the just vacated stage.

The intention was unmistakable, and the tension in the audience could have been cut with a knife, yet the Soviet theatre artists in the audience did not find the political content of the play outrageous, or even remarkable. Instead, they wanted to talk about the dubious quality of both the script and the production. Indeed, on the basis of the visual images, the emotions portrayed on stage and my interpreter's whispered translation, I had to agree with their evaluation.

* * *

Running in repertory at the Moscow Art Theatre was *We, The Undersigned* by Alexandr Gelman. This extraordinary play (which examines corruption in the upper echelons of Russian bureaucracy) is by one of the country's senior playwrights, a modern-day Russian Shaw who specializes in finely crafted political and moral studies of the world around him. *We, The Undersigned* is a clever and witty play that, because theatre is so much more important and visible in Moscow than, say, in Toronto, became a major local political event by virtue of its very performance.

At a performance of the play in East Berlin, which I had seen one week before arriving in Moscow, the reaction in the house to the initial jokes about the KGB and the Communist Party had been hearty laughter, until one outraged spectator exclaimed loudly from the middle of the audience, "There is nothing to laugh at here!" The performance continued, but in a somewhat strained atmosphere.

* * *

Most Western theatre observers consider Lyubimov to be one of the most radical and creative of the contemporary Russian directors. His productions had always given the Russian authorities problems; a difficulty which he eventually solved (to everyone's satisfaction) by defecting to the west. Lyubimov has worked throughout Europe and now lives in Italy, where he runs a theatre.

Lyubimov's production of Moliere's *Tartuffe*, which premièred twenty years ago, is still in the repertoire of Moscow's Taganka Theatre, five years after his defection—the authorities have simply removed all mention of his name from the program credits! This *Tartuffe* blends a wide variety of performance styles with a great deal of original dialogue, and also introduces the characters of The King and The Cardinal. The result is a not-so-veiled parallel to the State censorship of plays in contemporary Russia, a topic which twenty years ago must have been considered quite brazen. Even today, all scripts performed in any theatre in Russia must be cleared by the "State Copyright Bureau" (VAAP). Consequently, the political content of Russian plays is often couched in historical allegory, or expressed through staging and characterization rather than in the actual spoken words of the play.

Also remaining in the repertoire of the Taganka is Lyubimov's swan song, his final Moscow production, Chekhov's *The Three Sisters*—a modern-dress version of the play which academics would call Brechtian, and others ... misguided.

The production opens with the side-wall of the theatre rolling back to reveal a contemporary Russian army band playing a piece of tear-jerking Russian kitsch: this is the artillery band in Chekhov's script. The romantic theme of this opening music weaves its way through the entire production. The acting style is about as anti-Stanislavskian as one could imagine, with a good portion of the monologues being directed at the audience, and the house lights going on and off for most of the play—convenient if you are trying to follow the cuts in an English version of the play-text!

The longing for change that the characters in *The Three Sisters* express had been updated from despairing under *fin de siècle* Czarism to a more contemporary Russian counterpart. So, when Olga, at the end of the play, says, "The years will pass, and we shall all be gone for good and quite forgotten.... But our sufferings may mean happiness for the people who come after us.... There'll be a time when peace and happiness reign in the world ...," the words take on a meaning relevant to today's Russia. Again, no director was credited in the program.

The entire production was a reflection of a world that seemed to have no order: lights switching on and off, acting styles spinning on a kopek, characters roughly hewn—there was absolutely no chance of the audience becoming at all engaged emotionally with what was going on on stage. It felt a little bit like watching a hockey game in which there were neither goals nor rules....

This evening of theatre was clearly important to the citizens of Moscow, who watched in silence. Yet the quality of the production gave credence to the rumour circulating in London (where Lyubimov has worked since defecting) that he had deliberately manipulated the Western press, suckering them into believing that he was a radical genius, so when he finally did defect, his market value and reputation had been grossly inflated, leading to work offers galore.

Also at the Moscow Art Theatre was a production of Chekhov's *Uncle Vanya*, which invited comparison to the recent Tarragon Theatre production. Here was the legacy of Stanislavsky manifest—a cast of Russia's theatre élite had both the original prompt book for research and years of accumulated character analysis to draw upon. And yet ... where in Toronto, Derek and Nora and Fiona had found a genuine life in the play and the climax had been hysterically funny, in Moscow the play seemed to roll along ponderously, and the audience did not laugh *even once*. There was simply none of the comic excess of human characterization which we associate with Chekhov.

* * *

As a guest of the Soviet section of the International Theatre Institute, one has hospitality lavished upon one: unlimited theatre tickets and interviews with any local theatre people one desires to meet. I spent some time with the Director of the National Theatre School, who was prepared to discuss their curriculum at great length, especially their plan for a training system which graduates over one thousand artists to guaranteed employment every year. (Our NTS in Montreal will graduate seven English-speaking actors this year.)

The director, a small, squat man with a great deal of space between his pupils and the back of his mind, was a former Deputy Minister of Culture, and clearly a man who had experienced power. With a lovely display of one-upmanship, he encouraged me to apply for a grant from their government, so that I might apprentice with a Russian director.

When asked how Russian theatre was going to avoid ossification, he outlined for me a scheme being initiated in Leningrad: the Ministry of Culture had appointed an Artistic Committee in every theatre, composed of actors, directors and technicians. These committees were to evaluate the work of the artists working in each company. Those assessed as not achieving the quality of work demanded by the collective would be asked to leave their company. (They would, however, be guaranteed employment elsewhere!)

Among others, I also spoke with Anatoly Vassilow, a Rasputin look-alike with a black beard and hair down to his shoulders, who clearly resented being summoned to talk theatre with some unknown Canadian artist. He is considered by the younger generation of Russian critics and directors to be the hope for the future of the art form. Asked to comment on the Leningrad plan described above, he snorted, "That's just changing your brand of soap powder ..." This razor-sharp, intense director, who quickly warmed up, maintained that the road to the future lay in the actors' being permitted to re-group according to common stylistic and theoretical aims, and inhabiting new performance spaces.

* * *

The curiosity of the Moscovites is extraordinary, and their love of talk insatiable. Inevitably, every night ends up with fifteen people sitting around a tiny kitchen table, arguing theatre and politics over vodka until three a.m., or with endless toasts to peace at the Actor's Club.

One cannot help but be overwhelmed by the vastness of the tradition and the depth of the theatre in Mother Russia, the variety, quality and experience of the actors, and the high degree of importance and respect granted them. Moscow has some thirty State-run theatres and a small but increasing number of fringe theatres in basements of housing estates. And every seat in every theatre is full for each performance! The paradox is, possibly, that while this situation builds security and confidence in the work, it also breeds complacency.

* * *

On arrival in Moscow, a fellow Torontonian had generously offered me a ride to the hotel in his cab. We hadn't been driving for more than a few minutes, when he pulled out a tiny, state-of-the-art tape recorder and started to "see" Russia—"The streets are dull and boring ... the people are dressed poorly ... soldiers everywhere ... cars are small and colourless ... the people all look unhappy ..." If you want to have your prejudices about Russian life confirmed it's a lot simpler and cheaper to buy a ticket to a reactionary film like *Rocky IV*.

Appendix B

[The following article about my attempt to visit Saratov appeared in the *Toronto Star*, March 16, 1989. Reprinted with permission—the *Toronto Star* Syndicate.]

Metro man victim of Soviet red tape

by Stephen Handelman

MOSCOW—A leading Toronto theatre director was a victim of "red tape" and bureaucratic bungling during a trip to the Soviet Union last month, a Moscow newspaper has charged.

Soviet visa officials prevented Guy Sprung, co-artistic director of the Canadian Stage Company in Toronto, from accepting an invitation to visit a theatre in the Volga River town on Saratov, the government newspaper Isvestia said.

In a story apparently intended to embarrass Soviet officialdom, the paper documented Sprung's treatment at the hands of OVIR, the visa registration department which plays a large part in the lives of foreigners as well as Soviet citizens who want to travel abroad.

'Complete indifference'

Saratov, more than 500 kilometres (300 miles) southeast of Moscow, is located in a zone normally closed to Westerners for security reasons.

But local theatre people apparently believed they could win approval for Sprung's visit on the grounds it would lead to future artistic exchanges between Canada and the Soviet Union.

"Instead we were met with red tape, formalities and complete indifference to our problems," Alexander Dzekun, director of the Karl Marx theatre in Saratov, told Isvestia.

The disclosure of what happened to Sprung represents a startling departure even in the age of glasnost (openness). Soviet newspapers have only recently begun to complain about the existence of "closed zones" where foreigners and occasionally even Soviet citizens cannot travel.

Most of the zones are believed to be located near military installations.

The Soviet foreign ministry announcement yesterday of the expulsion of a U.S. military attache, in retaliation for a similar move by Washington last week, alleged the American had "attempted to penetrate a closed area."

Canadian sources confirmed the Sprung case yesterday, noting that the director was on a private visit and not connected with an official delegation. No complaint was lodged with the government, an embassy official told The Star.

Sprung was attending an international dramatic arts festival in Moscow when he received the invitation to visit the Karl Marx Theatre, considered one of the best in the country.

According to Isvestia, Sprung and his Soviet counterparts were to discuss bringing the Saratov troupe to Toronto.

Sprung, who was once invited to be guest director at Moscow's Pushkin Theatre, is a respected figure in the Soviet arts community.

"But instead of seeing the (Saratov) productions first-hand, he became a witness of another show, a bureaucratic show," the newspaper commented tartly.

Isvestia said permission for Sprung's visit had originally been granted at short notice after consultation with local Communist party officials and the KGB. Sprung was even told to pack for the trip.

'Degrading delays'

But another official from the local office of OVIR insisted she had to wait for orders from Moscow before issuing the correct papers, the newspaper said.

"There was a great deal of running about, phone calls and degrading delays over the next four days, until finally (Alexander) Dzekun was told he had gone about the process the wrong way," wrote Isvestia's Saratov correspondent, V. Nikolaeva.

Sprung confirmed the incident yesterday.

"There was good will on both sides but we couldn't seem to break through the red tape," he told The Star's Robert Crew. "But I'd certainly like to get to Saratov some day soon."

The Isvestia story appeared to be part of a growing campaign in the Soviet press against bureaucracy. But a foreigner's difficulties with the system have rarely been portrayed so sympathetically.

The story received prominent display on Page 1 of Monday's edition.

The newspaper concluded its account with some tongue-in-cheek advice to Saratov theatre officials, advising them to start now if they wanted to try inviting Sprung again.

"Perhaps over a period of several years, they'll succeed in breaking down the bureaucracy, indifference and mismanagement," wrote Nikolaeva. "Of course, the art of the theatre being so short-lived, the productions which interested the Canadian theatre company may have been taken off the repertoire.

"But that evidently wouldn't bother the bureaucrats."

Appendix C

[I received the following letter from Elena six weeks after I left Moscow.]

20 XII 1990
after the performance

Dear Guy,

I waited for your phone call but realized that it might not come so I decided to write a letter about the life of the play.

To begin with concretely: 1st act lasts 1 h. 30 min. (sometimes 1 h. 25 min.). 2nd act 1 hr. or 55 min. The attendance on the average is 75-80%, but sometimes we have full house. The play is received very well, especially by the young ones. I am surprised that there are no reviews, but it could be due to politico-theatrical games.

I made a new flute. In Masha's costume I made some alterations as you had wished.

Now about the actors: Lysander works best of all. He found many interesting things and is growing with each presentation.

Theseus played poorly and continues to play poorly. Yermakov is working well, but he sometimes drags the rhythm or lapses into a false self-importance. He listens carefully to criticism, though, and corrects his mistakes.

Maria Zubareva is working very well.

The mechanicals are working much better. I think it's because of the success they have with the public, especially in the last act.

The students are great and their work is noticed by all who watch the play.

Agapitov, Sergei—is the idol of the public. They say he's the pearl of the play. He works with pleasure.

I have succeeded in improving the lighting. They are working with greater accuracy and with bigger interest.

Some events could not be avoided. Biakova (Helena) became sick. Tanya and I replaced her with Skorokhodova and Hippolyta was replaced with Kara-Masco who plays the first fairy. Kara-Masco played very well, with precision and finesse. Each of her thoughts can be grasped. Great kid!

Skorokhodova did not spoil the play, as we pointed out the rough edges in the part, but to my thinking she is a stiff actress and very mannered.

So, Guy, this is how things are here. The play grew as it progressed and acquired liberty. The audience also contributed to it. Before the performance, at 5:30, we rehearse all the vocal numbers, and dances and the finale. It became a habit and now we are all used to doing it. Everything is going well with the music (thank God!).

While working on the Shakespeare play I got so used to you that I took your departure like a separation from a very close person. Too bad. Yet I hope just the same that it is not forever and that we will meet again.

Call me and write to me about everything that interests you and about your life.

> Once again, Merry Christmas
> May God take care of you.
> I embrace you. I miss you.
>
> Elena

Appendix D

[The following comments by audience members at the November 8, 1990 performance of *A Midsummer Night's Dream* were recorded by CBC Moscow and subsequently broadcast on CBC Radio Toronto. Prepared by Jennifer Clibbon at "The Arts Tonight" for CBC Stereo.]

"I came with my sixteen-year-old daughter. The first scene with the guns and soldiers didn't make sense to me. But then I was surprised by what came next. I thought the show was wonderful, wonderful. The teenage actors are great. It's nice to see this kind of style, like a rock opera. Very interesting, we sat enthralled the whole time and smiled."

"I think the director has done something unusual. For example, I imagined that we'd see a typical Shakespeare done the classical way. Well, I suppose it's a little unusual. Of course, it means one has to think a bit in order to understand what the parallels are."

"The last scene in the first act was amazing. With the McDonald's package, that was great.... When Puck finds a McDonald's package he opens it and throws it away in disgust. He finds a Russian bread bun, tea— and eats. The audience understands that he's relaxing in the Russian way. Interesting."

"Very dynamic and lots of music, lots of dance. We have few of these kind of dramatic musical shows. So it was a great pleasure to watch. Shakespeare is performed in Moscow theatres, but the more, the better, because it's a special thing."

"We're used to seeing the classical style. It's a little bit of a strange interpretation. Maybe for the young people it's good. But for people of my older age, I like, for example, *Much Ado About Nothing*, with King Lear ...

right? This is, well, not unusual. I guess we should accept it as something new ... of course the actors perform really well."

"I wasn't clear about what the symbolism of the shooting and soldiers was. I don't get the idea of the director. It has no connection to Shakespeare, there's nothing to refer to it in the text. I'm of the older generation, I'm 77 years old, I guess I can't really understand this new interpretation. It's probably something the young would understand better."

"The shooting might be connected to the Amazons, and there's a Greek myth about the war between the Amazons ... And there's love between the victors of the Amazons."

"I don't like the play."

"I've read this play, but in this contemporary style it's unusual ... and interesting."

"Well, it's clearly well directed, well thought out, good. But I think as a professional actress that the actors weren't always so strong in their roles ... they dance badly."

Appendix E

[The following sketches are some of the original designs for the set and costumes.]

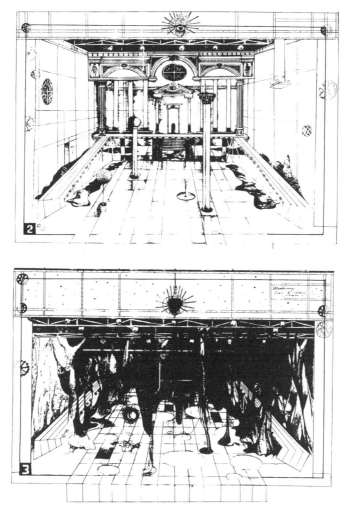

The set

Theseus (r) and a soldier

Hippolyta

Helena

Titania

Bottom

Puck

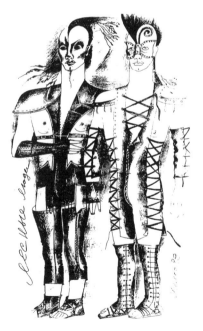

Two fairies

Karl Marx and Leon Trotsky
(only Trotsky appeared in the play)

About the authors

Born in Ottawa, **GUY SPRUNG** is considered one of Canada's foremost theatrical directors. He gained a national reputation for productions that included several premières: W.O. Mitchell's *Back to Beulah* (1976) and *The Black Bonspiel of Wullie MacCrimmon* (1980); David Fennario's *Nothing to Lose* (1976) and *Balconville* (1979); Rick Salutin's *Les Canadiens*; Anne Chislett's *Quiet in the Land* (1982); and both the 1979 national tour and the Toronto Free Theatre production of *Paper Wheat*.

In 1986–87 Sprung had a one-year interim appointment as artistic director of the Vancouver Playhouse. In 1986 he laid the groundwork for Toronto Free Theatre's merger with Toronto's Centrestage—culminating, in 1988, with the founding of the Canadian Stage Company, of which he was co-artistic director until his highly publicized firing in the fall of 1990. He is currently directing a docudrama and developing an international production entitled *Democracy!*

Former dramaturge of Toronto's Canadian Stage Company, **RITA MUCH** has taught English and Drama at the University of British Columbia and the University of Toronto. She recently served as Programming Chair of the Second International Women Playwrights Conference, held in Toronto in May 1991. She is the co-editor (with Judith Rudakoff) of *Fair Play* (Simon and Pierre) and is the editor of *Women on Women* (Blizzard Publishing), to be released in 1992.